3 /

The Observer's Pocket Series

AIRCRAFT

The Observer Books

The Observer's Book of

AIRCRAFT

COMPILED BY
WILLIAM GREEN

WITH SILHOUETTES BY
DENNIS PUNNETT

DESCRIBING 13/ AIRCRAFT
WITH 245 ILLUSTRATIONS

1976 Edition

FREDERICK WARNE & CO LTD
FREDERICK WARNE & CO INC
LONDON · NEW YORK

INTRODUCTION TO THE 1976 EDITION

By the time this 25th annual edition of *The Observer's Book of Aircraft* is published, fare-paying passengers on two of the world's principal airlines will be flying regularly at unprecedented speeds. Indeed, this year of 1976 will undoubtedly be recalled in the annals of aviation first and foremost as being that in which the era of supersonic air transportation was truly launched, for, in January, the Concorde, which first appeared in the pages of the *Oberver's Book* eight years ago, finally entered service with British Airways and Air France. True, its Soviet counterpart, the Tu-144, initiated a service a month earlier, on December 26, between Moscow and Alma Ata, but as it carried only "freight and mail", it stole nothing of the Concorde's thunder.

But if 1976 is to prove outstanding in aeronautical history for this epoch-marking development, there would seem little likelihood at the time of closing for press that it will also prove outstanding for the new aircraft types that will make their appearance during its 12 months. Indeed, the Western aircraft industries promise only one truly noteworthy newcomer, the highly innovative Boeing YC-14, which, expected to commence its flight test programme during the summer, will join the McDonnell Douglas YC-15 as a contender for the USAF's advanced military STOL transport (AMST) requirement. In so far as the East is concerned, the débutante of the year is likely to be the Ilyushin Il-86, an aircraft markedly less innovatory but nonetheless noteworthy in being the first Soviet airbus-type transport.

This paucity of entirely new aircraft types was also to be seen over the previous 12 months, for those revealed during the course of 1975 and making their appearance for the first time in the pages of the *Observer's Book* this year are restricted virtually to the Jugoslav–Romanian Orao light tactical aircraft, the Finnish Leko-70 primary trainer and the previously-mentioned YC-15, but provisional illustrations and details are included of the latest Soviet combat aircraft to attain service status, the variable-geometry Sukhoi Su-19 ground attack fighter, and the older aircraft types which occupy the bulk of the pages that follow, albeit frequently in modified form, are leavened with such "new" types as the Fuji KM-2B and Beech Turbo Mentor, derivatives of the original Beechcraft Mentor that first appeared 27 years ago, the Israeli Kfir fighter, perhaps best described as a *mélange* of French aerodynamic design and US engine technology, and the Atlas C4M Kudu of South African origin if not entirely of indigenous or original design.

As in past years, the *raison d'être* of this annual is to present in compact form the new aircraft types and variants of existing types that have appeared during the preceding 12 months or may be expected to appear during the year of currency of the volume. For those aircraft that the reader is most likely to *see*, the companion *Observer's Basic Aircraft Directories* are recommended.   WILLIAM GREEN

AERITALIA (FIAT) G.222

Country of Origin: Italy.

Type: General-purpose military transport.

Power Plant: Two 3,400 shp General Electric T64-P4D turboprops.

Performance: Max. speed, 329 mph (530 km/h) at sea level, 336 mph (540 km/h) at 15,000 ft (4 575 m); normal cruise, 224 mph (360 km/h) at 14,750 ft (4 500 m); range with 11,025-lb (5 000-kg) payload, 1,920 mls (3 250 km), with max. fuel, 3,262 mls (5 250 km); max. initial climb rate, 1,890 ft/min (9,6 m/sec).

Weights: Empty, 32,165 lb (14 590 kg); empty equipped, 33,950 lb (15 400 kg); max. take-off, 58,422 lb (26 500 kg).

Accommodation: Flight crew of three or four and seats for 44 fully-equipped troops or 40 paratroops. Alternative loads include 36 casualty stretchers, two jeep-type vehicles or equivalent freight.

Status: First of two prototypes flown July 18, 1970, followed by second prototype on July 22, 1971. An order for 12 aircraft for the Italian Air Force was placed in 1974 against planned procurement of 44, with first production aircraft rolled out on November 21, 1975, and two aircraft scheduled to be delivered early 1976. Two ordered by Argentina with option on a third.

Notes: Prototypes powered by CT64-820 turboprops and unpressurised, but the current production model has uprated T64-P4D turboprops and provision for pressurisation.

AERITALIA (FIAT) G.222

Dimensions: Span, 94 ft $5\frac{3}{4}$ in (28,80 m); length, 74 ft $5\frac{1}{2}$ in (22,70 m); height, 32 ft $1\frac{3}{4}$ in (9,80 m); wing area, 970·9 sq ft (90,2 m²).

AERMACCHI MB.339

Country of Origin: Italy.

Type: Two-seat trainer and light tactical aircraft.

Power Plant: One 4,000 lb (1 814 kg) Fiat-built Rolls-Royce Viper Mk 632–43 turbojet.

Performance: (Estimated) Max. speed, 558 mph (898 km/h) at 985 ft (300 m) or Mach 0·73, 508 mph (817 km/h) at 30,000 ft (9 145 m) or Mach 0·77; max. range (internal fuel), 1,093 mls (1 760 km); initial climb, 7,050 ft/min (35,8 m/sec).

Weights: Empty, 6,768 lb (3 070 kg); loaded (clean), 9,590 lb (4 350 kg); max. take-off, 12,500 lb (5 670 kg).

Armament: (Armament training and light strike) One 7,62-mm GAU-2B/A multi-barrel machine gun with 1,500 rounds or one 30-mm DEFA cannon with 120 rounds. Provision for up to 3,500 lb (1 587 kg) of external stores on six underwing stations.

Status: The first of two prototypes of the MB.339 scheduled to commence test programme during first half of 1976. Italian Air Force has a requirement for up to 100 aircraft to replace the MB.326 with initial production deliveries scheduled for 1977–78.

Notes: The MB.339 basic and advanced trainer is based on the airframe of late production versions of the MB.326 (see 1974 edition), incorporating the strengthened wing and centre section of the MB.326K single-seat light strike aircraft which, being optimised for low-level operation, provides a training role fatigue life of at least 10,000 hours. An interchangeable flush-fitting pod may be inserted in a bay beneath the rear seat, this containing gun armament or photo-reconnaissance equipment.

AERMACCHI MB.339

Dimensions: Span (over tip-tanks), 35 ft 7 in (10,85 m); length, 36 ft 0 in (10,97 m); height, 12 ft 10¼ in (3,92 m); wing area, 207·74 sq ft (19,30 m²).

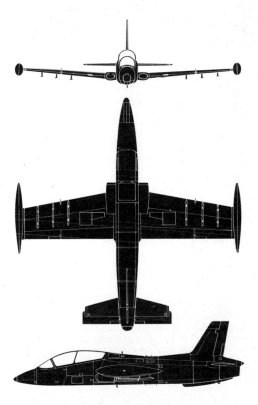

AERO L 39 ALBATROS

Country of Origin: Czechoslovakia.
Type: Tandem two-seat basic and advanced trainer.
Power Plant: One 3,792 lb (1 720 kg) Walter Titan (Ivchenko AI-25TL) turbofan.
Performance: (At 9,259 lb/4 200 kg) Max. speed, 438 mph (705 km/h) at sea level, 470 mph (757 km/h) at 16,405 ft (5 000 m), 457 mph (737 km/h) at 32,810 ft (10 000 m); initial climb, 4,330 ft/min (22 m/sec); time to 16,405 ft (5 000 m), 5 min, to 32,810 ft (10 000 m), 17 min; max. range (fuselage tanks only), 565 mls (910 km).
Weights: Empty equipped, 7,440 lb (3 375 kg); normal loaded, 9,259 lb (4 200 kg); max. take-off, 10,141 lb (4 600 kg).
Armament: (Weapon training) Two wing hard points for gun or rocket pods, or (L 39Z) four wing hard points for ASMs, 16-rocket pods or 20-mm cannon pods.
Status: First of five prototypes flown November 4, 1968, and first of 10 pre-production aircraft flown 1971, with first production deliveries (to Czech and Soviet air forces) commencing 1973.
Notes: Successor to the L 29 Delfin, the L 39 has entered service with the Czech and Soviet air arms, and a light strike variant, the L 39Z, is currently under development and has reportedly been ordered by Iraq, together with the standard training model. The L 39 is expected to be adopted as standard training equipment by all Warsaw Pact countries with the exception of Poland. The L 39 is the principal component of a training system which includes a specially-designed flight simulator (TL-39), a pilot ejection ground training simulator and vehicle-mounted mobile automatic test equipment.

AERO L 39 ALBATROS

Dimensions: Span, 31 ft 0½ in (9,46 m); length, 40 ft 5 in (12,32 m); height, 15 ft 5⅘ in (4,72 m); wing area, 202·36 sq ft (18,8 m²).

AÉROSPATIALE SN 601 CORVETTE

Country of Origin: France.

Type: Light business executive transport.

Power Plant: Two 2,310 lb (1 048 kg) Pratt & Whitney (Canada) JT15D-4 turbofans.

Performance: Max. cruise, 472 mph (760 km/h) at 29,530 ft (9 000 m); econ. cruise, 351 mph (565 km/h) at 37,730 ft (11 500 m); range (with 12 passengers and reserves), 915 mls (1 470 km); max. range (with tip-tanks), 1,555 mls (2 500 km); max. climb rate, 3,000 ft/min (15,24 m/sec); service ceiling, 41,000 ft (12 500 m).

Weights: Empty equipped, 7,695 lb (3 490 kg); max. take-off, 13,550 lb (6 600 kg).

Accommodation: Crew of one or two on flight deck and various alternative cabin arrangements for six to 14 passengers.

Status: Prototype (SN 600) flown July 16, 1970, followed by first of two pre-series aircraft (SN 601) on December 20, 1972. First of initial production series of five flown November 9, 1973, customer deliveries commencing in September 1974.

Notes: The current production version of the Corvette is the SN 601 described above, but a projected version, the SN 602, will be powered by two 2,755 lb (1 250 kg) SNECMA/Turboméca Larzac 03 turbofans. A stretched version of the basic design with accommodation for up to 18 passengers was discontinued during 1975. The Corvette is being offered for the military crew training role, for the aeromedical task with accommodation for three stretchers and two medical attendants, for aerial photography and for radio aids calibration.

12

AÉROSPATIALE SN 601 CORVETTE

Dimensions: Span, 42 ft 2⅔ in (12,87 m), with tip tanks, 45 ft 0 in (13,72 m); length, 45 ft 4 in (13,82 m); height, 13 ft 10 in (4,23 m); wing area, 236·8 sq ft (22,00 m²).

AIRBUS A300B4

Country of Origin: International consortium.

Type: Medium-haul commercial transport.

Power Plant: Two 51,000 lb (23 130 kg) General Electric CF6-50C turbofans.

Performance: Max. cruise, 586 mph (943 km/h) at 25,000 ft (7 620 m); econ. cruise, 554 mph (891 km/h) at 31,000 ft (9 450 m); long-range cruise, 585 mph (941 km/h) at 33,000 ft (10 060 m); range with max. payload, 2,530 mls (4 074 km); max. range (with 47,690-lb/21 633-kg payload), 4,014 mls (6 315 km).

Weights: Operational empty, 192,700 lb (87 409 kg); max. take-off, 330,700 lb (150 000 kg).

Accommodation: Flight crew of three and various arrangements for 220–300 passengers, or high-density arrangement for 345 passengers in nine-abreast seating.

Status: First and second A300Bs (dimensionally to B1 standard) flown October 28, 1972, and February 5, 1973, respectively, with third A300B (to B2 standard) flying on June 28, 1973. First A300B to B4 standard flown December 26, 1974. Orders and options for 52 placed by beginning of 1976 when production of 58 authorised with long-lead items for further 26.

Notes: The A300B is manufactured by a consortium comprising Aérospatiale (France), Deutsche Airbus (Federal Germany), Hawker Siddeley (UK) and Fokker-VFW (Netherlands). The first and second aircraft (A300B1s) had a 167 ft 2¼ in (50,97 m) fuselage, and the current B2 and B4 are dimensionally similar to each other, the latter having increased weights and fuel capacity, and wing leading-edge Krueger flaps to improve take-off performance.

AIRBUS A300B4

Dimensions: Span, 147 ft 1¼ in (44,84 m); length, 175 ft 11 in (53,62 m); height, 54 ft 2 in (16,53 m); wing area, 2·799 sq ft (260,0 m²).

AIR METAL AM-C111

Country of Origin: Federal Germany.

Type: Light STOL utility transport.

Power Plant: Two 1,174 eshp Pratt & Whitney (Canada) PT6A-45 turboprops.

Performance: (Estimated for Series 100) Max. cruise, 258 mph (416 km/h) at sea level, 254 mph (409 km/h) at 20,000 ft (6 100 m); max. payload range (with 4,940 lb/2 240 kg), 373 mls (600 km); max. fuel range (with 1,800 lb/820 kg), 1,677 mls (2 700 km); initial climb, 2,000 ft/min (10,2 m/sec); service ceiling, 26,900 ft (8 200 m).

Weights: Empty, 8,000 lb (3 630 kg); max. take-off, 14,990 lb (6 800 kg).

Accommodation: Flight crew of two and standard seating for 24 passengers.

Status: Prototype scheduled to commence flight test programme during first half of 1976. Licence manufacture to be undertaken in Turkey by new factory to be established at Kayseri.

Notes: Air Metal proposes to build small series of production aircraft as pattern machines and subsequently concentrate on sub-assembly kits for assembly by licensees. Projected developments include the Series 100HD, a high-density version with accommodation for 30 passengers, the pressurised Series 200, and the Series 300 and 400, respectively unpressurised and pressurised versions with provision for aft loading. The Series 100S, 200S, 300S and 400S embody a small fuselage stretch, and the Series 200SP and 400SP are special performance versions for the Turkish Air Force.

16

AIR METAL AM-C111

Dimensions: Span, 62 ft 11½ in (19,20 m); length, 53 ft 7´ in (16,34 m); height, 8 ft 0½ in (2,45 m); wing area, 408·56 sq ft (37,96 m²).

ANTONOV AN-28

Country of Origin: USSR.

Type: Light STOL general-purpose transport and feederliner.

Power Plant: Two 960 shp Glushenkov TVD-10A turbo-props.

Performance: Max. cruise, 217 mph (350 km/h); range with max. payload (3,306 lb/1 500 kg), 620 mls (1 000 km); initial climb rate, 2,360 ft/min (11,99 m/sec).

Weights: Empty equipped, 7,826 lb (3 550 kg); max. take-off, 12,566 lb (5 700 kg).

Accommodation: Normal flight crew of two and provision for maximum of 15 passengers in three-abreast seating (two to starboard and one to port), the seats folding back against the walls when the aircraft is employed in the freighter or mixed passenger/freight roles. Alternative versions provide for six or seven passengers in an executive layout and an aeromedical version accommodates six stretchers and a medical attendant.

Status: Initial prototype (An-14M) flown September 1969, its official flight testing being completed in 1972. A production prototype was tested with 810 shp Isotov TVD-850 turboprops (having meanwhile been redesignated An-28), this being re-engined with Glushenkov TVD-10As with which it flew in April 1975. Production deliveries are expected to commence during the course of 1976.

Notes: Essentially a scaled-up, turboprop-powered derivative of the piston-engined An-14, the An-28 has suffered a somewhat protracted gestation owing to delays in the development of suitable turboprops. The An-28 is being proposed for parachute training, geological survey, fire fighting, rescue operations and agricultural tasks.

ANTONOV AN-28

Dimensions: Span, 72 ft 2⅛ in (22,00 m); length, 42 ft 6⅞ in (12,98 m); height, 15 ft 1 in (4,60 m).

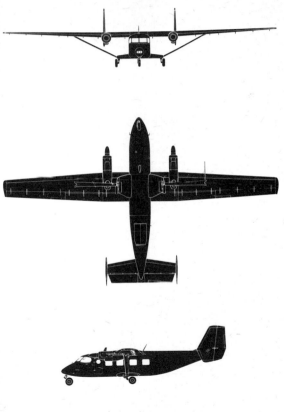

19

ANTONOV AN-30 (CLANK)

Country of Origin: USSR.

Type: Aerial survey aircraft.

Power Plant: Two 2,820 ehp Ivchenko AI-24T turboprops and one 1,764 lb (800 kg) Tumansky RU-19A-300 auxiliary turbojet.

Performance: Max. speed, 323 mph (520 km/h) at 19,685 ft (6 000 m); normal cruise, 264 mph (425 km/h); initial climb, 1,575 ft/min (8,0 m/sec); service ceiling, 27,230 ft (8 300 m); range, 1,616 mls (2 600 km); endurance, 6 hrs.

Weights: Empty equipped, 32,408 lb (14 700 kg); max. take-off, 50,706 lb (23 000 kg).

Accommodation: Standard crew of seven, including pilot, co-pilot, navigator, engineer and three photographers/ systems operators.

Status: The prototype An-30 initiated its flight test programme mid-1973 and the production model entered service with Aeroflot during the course of 1975.

Notes: The An-30 is a specialised aerial survey derivative of the An-24RT which, in turn, is a specialised freighter version of the An-24V *Seriiny II* (see 1969 edition) commercial transport. For the primary task of aerial photography for mapmaking, the An-30 is provided with four large survey cameras, and hatches permit the use of laser, thermographic, gravimetric, magnetic and geophysical sensors. The An-30 may also be used for microwave radiometer survey or mineral prospecting. Equipment includes a computer into which is fed a pre-programmed flight path, the computer subsequently controlling aircraft speed, altitude and course throughout the mission.

ANTONOV AN-30 (CLANK)

Dimensions: Span, 95 ft 9½ in (29,20 m); length, 79 ft 7⅛ in (24,26 m); height, 27 ft 3½ in (8,32 m); wing area, 807·1 sq ft (74,98 m²).

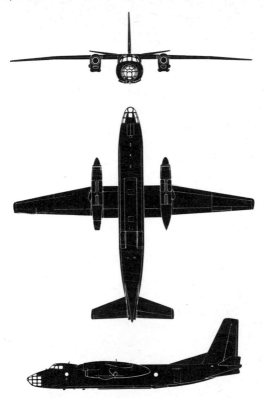

ATLAS C4M KUDU

Country of Origin: South Africa.

Type: Light STOL utility transport.

Power Plant: One 340 hp Piaggio-built Avco Lycoming GSO-480-B1B3 six-cylinder horizontally-opposed engine.

Performance: Max. speed, 161 mph (260 km/h) at 8,000 ft (2 440 m); max. continuous cruise, 144 mph (232 km/h) at 10,000 ft (3 050 m); econ. cruise, 121 mph (195 km/h); max. range, 806 mls (1 297 km).

Weights: Empty, 2,645 lb (1 200 kg); max. take-off, 4,497 lb (2 040 kg).

Accommodation: Pilot and co-pilot side-by-side with four individual passenger seats in pairs or two three-passenger bench-type seats. Space for up to 1,235 lb (560 kg) of freight with passenger seats removed.

Status: Prototype flown on 16 February 1974 with production deliveries against order from Light Aircraft Command of South African Air Force commencing late 1975.

Notes: The C4M Kudu has been developed by the Atlas Aircraft Corporation in collaboration with Aermacchi and possesses considerable commonality with the Aeritalia-Aermacchi AM-3C light surveillance and forward air control aircraft (see 1974 edition) which serves with the SAAF as the Bosbok (Bushbuck), mating the wings, tail assembly, undercarriage and power plant of this type with an essentially similar box-like fuselage to that of the Lockheed-Aermacchi AL.60 utility aircraft from which the AM-3C was originally derived. The Kudu is suitable for casevac, supply dropping and aerial survey roles.

ATLAS C4M KUDU

Dimensions: Span, 42 ft 7⅝ in (13,00 m); length, 29 ft 8 in (9,04 m); height, 9 ft 0 in (2,74 m); wing area, 225·1 sq ft (20,91 m²).

BAC ONE-ELEVEN 475

Country of Origin: United Kingdom.

Type: Short- to medium-range commercial transport.

Power Plant: Two 12,550 lb (5 692 kg) Rolls-Royce Spey 512-14-DW turbofans.

Performance: Max. cruise, 548 mph (882 km/h) at 21,000 ft (6 400 m); econ. cruise, 507 mph (815 km/h) at 25,000 ft (7 620 m); range with reserves for 230 mls (370 km) diversion and 45 min, 2,095 mls (3 370 km), with capacity payload, 1,590 mls (2 560 km).

Weights: Basic operational, 51,814 lb (23 502 kg); max. take-off, 92,000 lb (41 730 kg).

Accommodation: Basic flight crew of two and up to 89 passengers. Typical arrangement provides for 16 first- (four-abreast) and 49 tourist-class (five-abreast) passengers.

Status: Aerodynamic prototype of One-Eleven 475 flown August 27, 1970 followed by first production model on April 5, 1971, with certification and first production deliveries following in June. Total of 220 examples of all versions of the One-Eleven ordered by beginning of 1976.

Notes: The One-Eleven 475 combines the standard fuselage of the Series 400 with the redesigned wing and uprated engines of the Series 500 (see 1970 edition), coupling these with a low-pressure undercarriage to permit operation from gravel or low-strength sealed runways. The One-Eleven prototype flew on August 20, 1963, production models including the physically similar Series 200 and 300 with 10,330 lb (4 686 kg) Spey 506s and 11,400 lb (5 170 kg) Spey 511s, the Series 400 modified for US operation, and the Series 500 which is similar to the 475 apart from the fuselage and undercarriage. A passenger/cargo version of the 475 for the Sultan of Oman's Air Force is illustrated.

BAC ONE-ELEVEN 475

Dimensions: Span, 93 ft 6 in (28,50 m); length, 93 ft 6 in (28,50 m); height, 24 ft 6 in (7,47 m); wing area, 1,031 sq ft (95,78 m²).

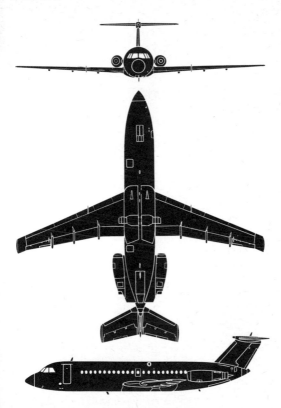

BAC-AÉROSPATIALE CONCORDE

Countries of Origin: United Kingdom and France.
Type: Long-range supersonic commercial transport.
Power Plant: Four 38,050 lb (17 259 kg) reheat Rolls-Royce/SNECMA Olympus 593 Mk. 602 turbojets.
Performance: Max. cruise, 1,354 mph (2 179 km/h) at 51,300 ft (15 635 m) or Mach 2·05; range with max. fuel (22,250-lb/10 092-kg payload and FAR reserves), 3,915 mls (6 300 km), with max. payload (28,000 lb/12 700 kg) at Mach 0·93 at 30,000 ft (9 145 m), 3,063 mls (4 930 km), at Mach 2·05, 3,869 mls (6 226 km); initial climb rate, 5,000 ft/min (25,4 m/sec); service ceiling (approx.), 60,000 ft (18 300 m).
Weights: Operational empty, 174,750 lb (79 265 kg); max. take-off, 400,000 lb (181 435 kg).
Accommodation: Normal flight crew of three and one-class seating for 128 passengers. Alternative high-density arrangement for 144 passengers.
Status: First and second prototypes flown March 2 and April 9, 1969, respectively. First of two pre-production aircraft flew December 17, 1971, and the first production example following on December 6, 1973, this having been joined by five others by the beginning of 1976 when 10 additional Concordes were under construction.
Notes: The Concorde began to operate its first fare-paying passengers in January 1976, services being initiated simultaneously by British Airways and Air France, these airlines having five and four Concordes on order respectively. Preliminary purchase agreements have been signed by China's CAAC (three) and Iran Air (two plus one on option).

BAC-AÉROSPATIALE CONCORDE

Dimensions: Span, 83 ft 10 in (25,56 m); length, 202 ft 3$\frac{3}{8}$ in (61,66 m); height, 37 ft 1 in (11,30 m); wing area, 3,856 sq ft (358,25 m²).

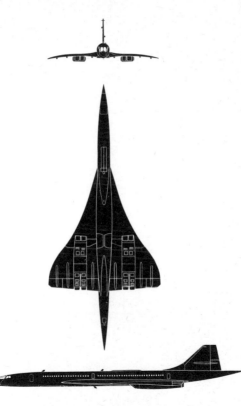

BEECHCRAFT MODEL 76

Country of Origin: USA.

Type: Light cabin monoplane.

Power Plant: Two 180 hp Avco Lycoming 0-360 series six-cylinder horizontally-opposed engines.

Performance: Max. cruise speed, 185 mph (298 km/h); range (with 45 min reserves), 800+ mls (1 287+ km).

Weights: No details available for publication.

Accommodation: Four seats in pairs with dual controls as standard.

Status: Prototype flown late summer of 1974 as the PD 289. Decision to launch production taken autumn 1975 with deliveries scheduled to commence in October 1977.

Notes: Bearing a close relation to the single-engined Sierra 200 and utilising some common structural components, the Model 76 will employ a honeycomb-bonded wing in production form; other changes from the prototype (illustrated here) include the replacement of the manually-operated by electrically-operated flaps, the introduction of electrically-operated trim tabs and the provision of a new oleo undercarriage shock-absorbing system. Doors are provided in both sides of the cabin with a third door giving access to a baggage compartment. The Model 76 is the second Beechcraft type to adopt a T-tail arrangement, having been preceded by the Super King Air 200.

BEECHCRAFT MODEL 76

Dimensions: Span, 38 ft 0 in (11,59 m); length, 29 ft 5 in (8,96 m); height, 8 ft 11 in (2,71 m).

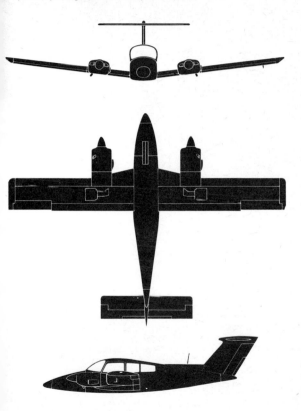

BEECHCRAFT KING AIR B100

Country of Origin: USA.

Type: Light business executive transport.

Power Plant: Two 715 shp Garrett AiResearch TPE 331-6-252B turboprops (derated from 840 shp).

Performance: Max. cruise (at 10,500 lb/4 762 kg), 306 mph (493 km/h) at 10,000 ft (3 050 m), 297 mph (478 km/h) at 21,000 ft (6 400 m); range (with reserves), 1,515 mls (2 438 km); initial climb, 1,985 ft/min (10,1 m/sec); service ceiling, 25,200 ft (7 680 m).

Weights: Empty, 7,127 lb (3 233 kg); max. take-off, 11,800 lb (5 352 kg).

Accommodation: Pilot and six to 13 passengers according to cabin arrangement.

Status: The B100 version of the King Air was certificated in November 1975, and customer deliveries commenced in January 1976.

Notes: The B100 is the latest addition to the King Air range of business aircraft and differs from the A100 (680 ehp Pratt & Whitney (Canada) PT6A-28 turboprops—see 1972 edition)—primarily in the type of engine installed. Production of the King Air A100 continues in parallel, together with the smaller-capacity King Air C90 (550 ehp PT6A-20s) and E90 (550 ehp PT6A-28s derated from 680 ehp), these having a wing span and overall length of 50 ft 3 in (15,32 m) and 35 ft 6 in (10,82 m) respectively.

BEECHCRAFT KING AIR B100

Dimensions: Span, 45 ft 10½ in (13,99 m); length, 39 ft 11¼ in (12,18 m); height, 15 ft 4¼ in (4,68 m); wing area, 279·7 sq ft (25,88 m²).

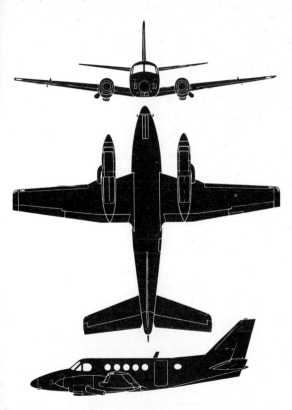

BEECHCRAFT SUPER KING AIR 200

Country of Origin: USA.

Type: Light business executive transport.

Power Plant: Two 850 shp Pratt & Whitney (Canada) PT6A-41 turboprops.

Performance: Max. cruise, 333 mph (536 km/h) at 12,000 ft (3 655 m), 320 mph (515 km/h) at 25,000 ft (7 620 m); max. range, 1,840 mls (2 961 km) at 27,000 ft (8 230 m) at max. cruise, 2,045 mls (3 290 km) at max. range cruise; initial climb, 2,450 ft/min (12,44 m/sec); service ceiling, 32,300 ft (9 845 m).

Weights: Empty equipped, 7,650 lb (3 470 kg); max. take-off, 12,500 lb (5 670 kg).

Accommodation: Flight crew of two and standard arrangement of six individual seats in main cabin with an optional eight-passenger arrangement. High-density configuration available.

Status: Prototype Super King Air flown October 27, 1972, with second example following on December 15. Customer deliveries commenced March 1974.

Notes: The Super King Air 200 is the fourth aircraft in the King Air range and differs from the King Air B100 (see pages 30–31) primarily in having increased wing span, higher cabin pressure differential, increased fuel tankage and a T-tail arrangement. Thirty Super King Air A200s (with 750 hp PT6A-38s) are being delivered to the USAF as C-12As and 40 to the US Army as U-25A Hurons.

BEECHCRAFT SUPER KING AIR 200

Dimensions: Span, 54 ft 6 in (16,60 m); length, 43 ft 9 in (13,16 m); height, 14 ft 11½ in (4,54 m); wing area, 303 sq ft (28,1 m²).

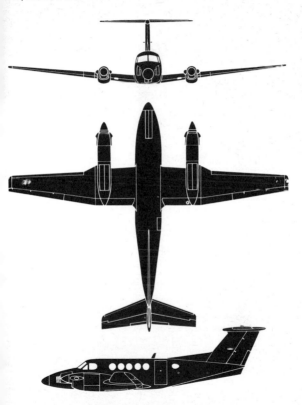

BEECHCRAFT T-34C TURBO MENTOR

Country of Origin: USA.
Type: Tandem two-seat primary trainer.
Power Plant: One 715 snp (derated to 400 shp) Pratt & Whitney (Canada) PT6A-45 turboprop.
Performance: Max. speed, 257 mph (414 km/h) at 17,500 ft (5 335 m); max. cruise, 247 mph (397 km/h) at 17,500 ft (5 335 m); range, 749 mls (1 205 km) at 20,000 ft (6 095 m); climb at 10,000 ft (3 050 m), 1,275 ft/min (6,48 m/sec); service ceiling, 30,000+ ft (9 150+ m).
Weights: Empty, 2,630 lb (1 194 kg); max. take-off, 4,274 lb (1 940 kg).
Status: First of two YT-34Cs (converted from T-34Bs) flown on September 21, 1974, and initial contracts placed for 93 T-34Cs for the US Navy against anticipated total requirement of 400 aircraft. First deliveries scheduled for March 1976.
Notes: The T-34C is an updated derivative of the original Beechcraft Model 45 primary trainer, a turboprop replacing the Continental 0-470-13 six-cylinder horizontally-opposed engine. Production of the original model included 450 as the T-34A for the USAF and 423 as the T-34B for the US Navy. The turboprop of the T-34C is fitted with a torque limiter to restrict output and thus ensure long engine life and constant performance over a wide range of temperatures and altitudes. US Navy pilots will receive *ab initio* training on the T-34C before progressing to the Rockwell T-2C Buckeye and then to training versions of operational aircraft.

BEECHCRAFT T-34C TURBO MENTOR

Dimensions: Span, 33 ft 4 in (10,17 m); length, 28 ft 8½ in (8,75 m); height, 9 ft 10 in (3,00 m); wing area, 179·9 sq ft (16,71 m²).

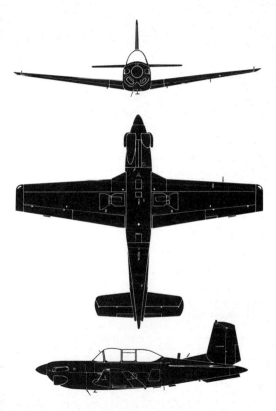

BELLANCA 19-25 SKYROCKET II

Country of Origin: USA.

Type: Light cabin monoplane.

Power Plant: One 435 hp Continental GTSIO-520-F six-cylinder horizontally-opposed engine.

Performance: Max. speed, 301 mph (485 km/h) at 19,000 ft (5 790 m); cruise (75% power), 261 mph (420 km/h) at 15,000 ft (4 570 m), (65% power), 250 mph (402 km/h); range (75% power), 1,215 mls (1 955 km), (65% power), 1,465 mls (2 355 km); initial climb, 1,890 ft/min (9,60 m/sec); service ceiling, 30,000 ft (9 150 m).

Weights: Empty, 2,150 lb (975 kg); max. take-off, 3,775 lb (1 712 kg).

Accommodation: Pilot and five passengers in pairs of individual seats.

Status: Prototype flown in May 1975.

Notes: Developed by the Bellanca Aircraft Engineering Corp—which has no connection with the Bellanca Aircraft Corporation which manufactures such types as the Scout and Super Viking (see 1975 edition)—to the designs of the late Giuseppe Bellanca, the Skyrocket II makes extensive use of glassfibre composite construction with moulded, load-bearing skins. The basic moulded components comprise inner and outer glassfibre skins epoxy-bonded to an aluminium honeycomb core, resulting in exceptionally smooth surfaces and, allegedly, better strength-to-weight ratio than aluminium. The fuselage is moulded in two halves with integral fin and wing and tailplane roots, and the wings are moulded in two half-shells with two glassfibre spars. Fuel is carried in integral tanks in each wing.

BELLANCA 19-25 SKYROCKET II

Dimensions: Span, 35 ft 0 in (10,67 m); length, 28 ft 11 in (8,81 m); height, 9 ft 3 in (2,82 m); wing area, 182·6 sq ft (16,96 m²).

BOEING MODEL 707-320C

Country of Origin: USA.
Type: Medium- to long-haul commercial transport.
Power Plant: Four 19,000 lb (8 618 kg) Pratt & Whitney JT3D-7 turbofans.
Performance: Max. cruise, 593 mph (956 km/h) at 30,000 ft (9 145 m); econ. cruise, 550 mph (885 km/h) at 35,000 ft (10 670 m); long-range cruise, 532 mph (856 km/h); range (max. payload of 84,000 lb/38 100 kg and no reserves), 4,300 mls (6 920 km), (max. fuel and no reserves), 7,475 mls (12 030 km).
Weights: Operational empty (passenger), 146,000 lb (66 224 kg), (cargo), 138,610 lb (62 872 kg); max. take-off, 333,600 lb (151 315 kg).
Accommodation: Max. accommodation for 219 economy-class passengers, but typical arrangement has 14 first-class and 133 coach-class seats.
Status: The prototype Model 707 first flew on July 15, 1954, the first production aircraft following on December 20, 1957. Production in a variety of versions .has since continued and was running at one per month at the beginning of 1976, when sales of the Model 707 (and the Model 720 derivative) totalled approximately 920 and only the 707-320C was being offered.
Notes: The Model 707-320C has been sold in larger numbers than any version of the basic design, some 330 having been delivered or being on order at the beginning of 1976. It is offered in convertible (cargo or mixed cargo—passenger) or all-cargo form, the latter having passenger facilities eliminated.

BOEING MODEL 707-320C

Dimensions: Span, 145 ft 9 in (44,42 m); length, 152 ft 11 in (46,61 m); height, 42 ft 5 in (12,93 m); wing area, 3,050 sq ft (283,4 m²).

BOEING MODEL 727-200

Country of Origin: USA.

Type: Short- to medium-range commercial transport.

Power Plant: Three 14,500 lb (6 577 kg) Pratt & Whitney JT8D-9 turbofans (with 15,000 lb/6 804 kg JT8D-11s or 15,500 lb/7 030 kg JT8D-15s as options).

Performance: Max. speed, 621 mph (999 km/h) at 20,500 ft (6 250 m); max. cruise, 599 mph (964 km/h) at 24,700 ft (7 530 m); econ. cruise, 570 mph (917 km/h) at 30,000 ft (9 145 m); range with 26,400-lb (11 974-kg) payload and normal reserves, 2,850 mls (4 585 km), with max. payload (41,000 lb/18 597 kg), 1,845 mls (2 970 km).

Weights: Operational empty (basic), 97,525 lb (44 235 kg), (typical), 99,000 lb (44 905 kg); max. take-off, 208,000 lb (94 347 kg).

Accommodation: Crew of three on flight deck and six-abreast seating for 163 passengers in basic arrangement with max. seating for 189 passengers.

Status: First Model 727-100 flown February 9, 1963, with first delivery (to United) following October 29, 1963. Model 727-200 flown July 27, 1967, with first delivery (to Northeast) on December 11, 1967. Deliveries from mid-1972 have been of the so-called "Advanced 727-200" (to which specification refers and illustrations apply) and a total of approximately 1,230 Model 727s had been ordered by the beginning of 1976 when production was running at seven per month.

Notes: The Model 727-200 is a "stretched" version of the 727-100 (see 1972 edition). Deliveries of the "Advanced 727" with JT8D-17 engines of 16,000 lb (7 257 kg), permitting an increase of 3,500 lb (1 587 kg) in payload, began (to Mexicana) in June 1974. The proposed Model 727-300 with a 15-ft (4,57-m) longer fuselage, modified wing with Krueger flaps and extended wingtips, and a gross weight in excess of 210,000 lb (95 255 kg), was indefinitely shelved during 1975.

BOEING MODEL 727-200

Dimensions: Span, 108 ft 0 in (32,92 m); length, 153 ft 2 in (46,69 m); height, 34 ft 0 in (10,36 m); wing area, 1,700 sq ft (157,9 m²).

BOEING MODEL 737-200

Country of Origin: USA.

Type: Short-haul commercial transport.

Power Plant: Two 14,500 lb (6 577 kg) Pratt & Whitney JT8D-9 turbofans.

Performance: Max. speed, 586 mph (943 km/h) at 23,500 ft (7 165 m); max. cruise (at 90,000 lb/40 823 kg), 576 mph (927 km/h) at 22,600 ft (6 890 m); econ. cruise, 553 mph (890 km/h) at 30,000 ft (9 145 m); range (max. fuel and reserves), 2,530 mls (4 075 km), (max. payload of 34,790 lb/ 15 780 kg and reserves), 2,370 mls (3 815 km).

Weights: Operational empty, 60,210 lb (27 310 kg); max. take-off, 115,500 lb (52 390 kg).

Accommodation: Flight crew of two and up to 130 passengers in six-abreast seating with alternative arrangement for 115 passengers.

Status: Model 737 initially flown on April 9, 1967, with first deliveries (737-100 to Lufthansa) same year. Stretched 737-200 flown on August 8, 1967, with deliveries (to United) in 1968. Total sales exceeded 460 (including 19 -200s delivered to USAF as T-43A navigational trainers—see 1975 edition) by the beginning of 1976 when production was running at four-five per month.

Notes: All aircraft delivered since May 1971 have been completed to the so-called "Advanced 737-200/C/QC" standard embodying improvements in range and short-field performance. A further stretched version, the 737-300, has been studied, but no decision to proceed with this has been taken.

BOEING MODEL 737-200

Dimensions: Span, 93 ft 0 in (28,35 m); length, 100 ft 0 in (30,48 m); height, 37 ft 0 in (11,28 m); wing area, 980 sq ft (91,05 m²).

BOEING MODEL 747-200B

Country of Origin: USA.

Type: Long-range large-capacity commercial transport.

Power Plant: Four 47,000 lb (21 320 kg) Pratt & Whitney JT9D-7W turbofans.

Performance: Max. speed at 600,000 lb (272 155 kg), 608 mph (978 km/h) at 30,000 ft (9 150 m); long-range cruise, 589 mph (948 km/h) at 35,000 ft (10 670 m); range with max. fuel and FAR reserves, 7,080 mls (11 395 km), with 79,618-lb (36 114-kg) payload, 6,620 mls (10 650 km); cruise ceiling, 45,000 ft (13 715 m).

Weights: Operational empty, 361,216 lb (163 844 kg); max. take-off, 775,000 lb (351 540 kg).

Accommodation: Normal flight crew of three and basic accommodation for 66 first-class and 308 economy-class passengers. Alternative layouts for 447 or 490 economy-class passengers nine- and 10-abreast respectively.

Status: First Model 747-100 flown on February 9, 1969, and first commercial services (by Pan American) inaugurated January 22, 1970. The first Model 747-200 (747B), the 88th aircraft off the assembly line, flown October 11, 1970. Some 300 of all versions had been ordered by the beginning of 1976.

Notes: Principal versions are the -100 and -200 series, the latter having greater fuel capacity and increased maximum take-off weight, convertible passenger/cargo and all-cargo versions of the -200 series being designated 747-200C and 747-200F. The first production example of the latter flew on November 30, 1971. Deliveries of the Model 747SR, a short-range version of the 747-100 (to Japan Air Lines), began September 1973. The 747-200B was flown on June 26, 1973 with 51,000 lb (23 133 kg) General Electric CF6-50D engines, and the 52,500 lb (23 810 kg) CF6-50E is offered as an optional installation in the -200 series.

BOEING MODEL 747-200B

Dimensions: Span, 195 ft 8 in (59,64 m); length, 231 ft 4 in (70,51 m); height, 63 ft 5 in (19,33 m); wing area, 5,685 sq ft (528,15 m²).

BOEING MODEL 747SP

Country of Origin: USA.

Type: Long-haul commercial transport.

Power Plant: Four 46,950 lb (21 296 kg) Pratt & Whitney JT9D-7A turbofans.

Performance: Max. cruise, 594 mph (957 km/h) at 35,000 ft (10 670 m); econ. cruise, 570 mph (918 km/h) at 35,000 ft (10 670 m); long-range cruise, 555 mph (893 km/h); range (with max. payload of 97,080 lb/44 034 kg), 6,620 mls (10 650 km), (with max. fuel and 30,000-lb/13 608-kg payload), 9,570 mls (15 400 km).

Weights: Operational empty, 315,000 lb (140 878 kg); max. take-off, 660,000 lb (299 370 kg).

Accommodation: Flight crew of three and basic accommodation for 28 first-class and 288 economy-class passengers. Max. high-density arrangement for 360 passengers in 10-abreast seating.

Status: First production Model 747SP flown July 4, 1975, with first customer deliveries (to Pan Am) following early 1976. Fifteen ordered by beginning of 1976.

Notes: The SP (Special Performance) version of the Model 747 embodies a reduction in overall length of 47 ft 7 in (14,30 m) and retains a 90% commonality of components with the standard Model 747 (see pages 44–45). The Model 747SP is intended primarily for operation over long-range routes where traffic densities are insufficient to support the standard model. Apart from having a shorter fuselage, the Model 747SP has taller vertical tail surfaces with a double-hinged rudder and new trailing-edge flaps.

BOEING MODEL 747SP

Dimensions: Span, 195 ft 8 in (59,64 m); length, 184 ft 9 in (56,31 m); height, 65 ft 5 in (19,94 m); wing area, 5,685 sq ft (528,15 m²).

BOEING E-3A

Country of Origin: USA.

Type: Airborne warning and control system aircraft.

Power Plant: Four 21,000 lb (9 525 kg) Pratt & Whitney TF33-PW-100/100A turbofans.

Performance: No details have been released for publication, but max. and econ. cruise speeds are likely to be generally similar to those of the equivalent commercial Model 707-320B (i.e., 627 mph/1 010 km/h and 550 mph/886 km/h respectively). Mission requirement is for 7-hr search at 29,000 ft (8 840 m) at 1,150 mls (1 850 km) from base. Unrefuelled endurance, 11·5 hrs.

Weights: Approx. max. take-off, 330,000 lb (149 685 kg).

Accommodation: The E-3A will carry an operational crew of 17 which may be increased according to mission. The complement comprises a flight crew of four, a four-man systems maintenance team, a battle commander and an eight-man air defence operations team.

Status: First of two EC-137D development aircraft flown February 9, 1972. Three pre-production examples of the operational derivative, the E-3A (one using EC-137D airframe), were produced, with the first (the EC-137D conversion) having commenced its trials in February 1975, and the second following in July 1975. Deliveries commencing by the end of 1976 against initial production contract for six E-3As.

Notes: As part of a programme for the development of a new AWACS (Airborne Warning And Control System) aircraft for operation by the USAF from the mid 'seventies, two Boeing 707-320B transports were modified as EC-137D test-beds. These were employed during 1972 for competitive evaluation of the competing Hughes and Westinghouse radars, the latter having been selected as winning contender.

BOEING E-3A

Dimensions: Span, 145 ft 9 in (44,42 m); length, 152 ft 11 in (46,61 m); height, 42 ft 5 in (12,93 m); wing area, 3,050 sq ft (283,4 m²).

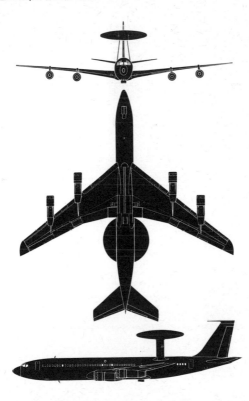

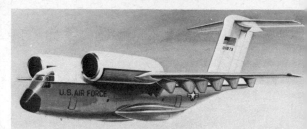

BOEING YC-14

Country of Origin: USA.

Type: Medium STOL tactical transport.

Power Plant: Two 49,000 lb (22 226 kg) General Electric CF6-50D turbofans.

Performance: (Estimated) Max. speed, 518 mph (834 km/h) at 30,000 ft (9 150 m); normal cruise, 472 mph (760 km/h); range (conventional operation) with max. payload (81,000 lb/36 740 kg), 1,150 mls (1 850 km), (STOL operation) with 27,000-lb (12 247-kg) payload, 460 mls (740 km).

Weights: Design max. take-off (STOL), 169,500 lb (76 880 kg), (conventional), 249,000 lb (112 945 kg).

Accommodation: Flight crew of three. Hold can accommodate all US Army vehicles up to and including the 62,000-lb (28 123-kg) extended-barrel self-propelled 8-in (20,3-cm) howitzer. Approximately 150 fully-equipped troops may be carried.

Status: First of two YC-14s scheduled to commence flight test programme summer 1976. The YC-14 will subsequently compete in a prototype fly-off contest with the McDonnell Douglas YC-15 (see pages 156–157).

Notes: The YC-14 is a contender for the USAF's advanced military STOL transport (AMST) requirement and embodies a number of innovative features such as a supercritical wing, the engines being mounted above and forward of the wing, leaving the undersurface uncluttered, wide-span leading- and trailing-edge flaps inducing the high-speed airflow from the engines to cling to the surface of the wing-flap system and directing it downward to generate powered lift.

BOEING YC-14

Dimensions: Span, 129 ft 0 in (39,32 m); length, 131 ft 8 in (40,13 m); height, 48 ft 2 in (14,68 m); wing area, 1,762 sq ft (163,7 m²).

BRITTEN-NORMAN BN-2A-8S ISLANDER

Country of Origin: United Kingdom.

Type: Light utility transport.

Power Plant: Two 260 hp Avco Lycoming O-540-E4C5 six-cylinder horizontally-opposed engines.

Performance: Max. speed, 170 mph (273 km/h) at sea level; cruise at 75% power, 160 mph (257 km/h) at 7,000 ft (2 140 m), at 67% power, 158 mph (253 km/h) at 9,000 ft (2 750 m), at 59% power, 154 mph (248 km/h) at 13,000 ft (3 960 m); range with standard fuel, 717 mls (1 154 km) at 160 mph (257 km/h), 870 mls (1 400 km) at 154 mph (248 km/h), tip tanks, 1,040 mls (1 674 km) at 160 mph (257 km/h), 1,263 mls (2 035 km) at 154 mph (248 km/h).

Weights: Empty equipped, 3,675 lb (1 667 kg); max. take-off, 6,600 lb (2 993 kg).

Accommodation: Flight crew of one or two and up to 10 passengers on pairs of bench-type seats.

Status: Prototype flown June 12, 1965, followed by first production aircraft on August 20, 1966. More than 750 ordered by beginning of 1976. Production transferred to Fairey SA in Belgium during 1973, the first Belgian-built example being delivered in December of that year, and 315 airframes being manufactured under contract by IRMA in Rumania. Eighty Islanders to be assembled (20) and part-manufactured (60) in the Philippines. Production was running at eight per month at the beginning of 1976.

Notes: The BN-2A-8S features a 45·5-in (1,15-m) longer nose to provide increased baggage space, an additional cabin window each side at the rear, and provision for an additional seat row. These changes, indicated by the suffix "S" (for Stretched), are being offered as customer options. A military multi-role version of the Islander is known as the Defender.

BRITTEN-NORMAN BN-2A-8S ISLANDER

Dimensions: Span, 49 ft 0 in (14,94 m); length, 39 ft 5¼ in (12,02 m); height, 13 ft 8 in (4,16 m); wing area, 325 sq ft (30,2 m²).

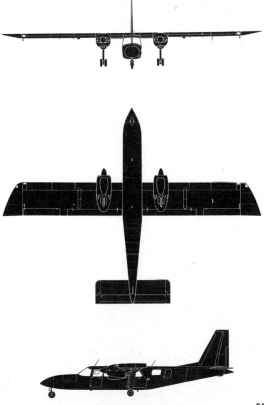

BRITTEN-NORMAN BN-2A MK. III-2 TRISLANDER

Country of Origin: United Kingdom.
Type: Light utility transport and feederliner.
Power Plant: Three 260 hp Avco Lycoming 0-540-E4C5 six-cylinder horizontally-opposed engines.
Performance: Max. speed, 183 mph (294 km/h) at sea level; cruise at 75% power, 176 mph (283 km/h) at 6,500 ft (1 980 m), at 67% power, 175 mph (282 km/h) at 9,000 ft (2 750 m); range with max. payload, 160 mls (257 km) at 170 mph (274 km/h), with 2,400-lb (1 089-kg) payload, 700 mls (1 127 km) at 175 mph (282 km/h).
Weights: Empty equipped, 5,700 lb (2 585 kg); max. take-off, 10,000 lb (4 536 kg).
Accommodation: Flight crew of one or two, and 16–17 passengers in pairs on bench-type seats.
Status: Prototype flown September 11, 1970, with production prototype flying on March 6, 1971. First production Trislander flown April 29, 1971, and first delivery (to Aurigny) following on June 29, 1971. Trislander production was transferred to Fairey SA at Gosselies, Belgium, late in 1972, and deliveries from the new line began early 1974. Some 60 Trislanders had been ordered by the beginning of 1976 when production was running at two per month.
Notes: The Trislander is a derivative of the Islander (see pages 52–53) with which it has 75% commonality. The wingtip auxiliary fuel tanks optional on the Islander have been standardised for the Trislander. An extended nose version (illustrated above), the Mk. III-2, flew on August 18, 1974.

BRITTEN-NORMAN BN-2A TRISLANDER

Dimensions: Span, 53 ft 0 in (16,15 m); length, 43 ft 9 in (13,33 m); height, 14 ft 2 in (4,32 m); wing area, 337 sq ft (31,25 m²).

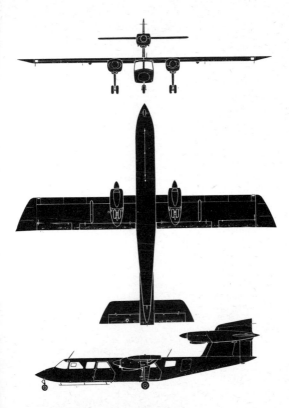

CASA C.212 AVIOCAR

Country of Origin: Spain.
Type: STOL utility transport, navigational trainer and photographic survey aircraft.
Power Plant: Two 776 eshp (715 shp) Garrett-AiResearch TPE 331-5-251C turboprops.
Performance: (At 13,889 lb/6 300 kg) Max. cruise, 243 mph (391 km/h) at 12,000 ft (3 658 m), 238 mph (383 km/h) at 5,000 ft (1 524 m); initial climb, 1,724 ft/min (8,76 m/sec); service ceiling, 24,605 ft (7 500 m); range with max. payload and reserves (30 min hold at 5,000 ft/ 1 524 m plus 5% take-off weight), 205 mls (330 km) at 12,500 ft (3 810 m), with max. fuel, 1,197 mls (1 927 km).
Weights: Empty equipped, 8,045 lb (3 650 kg); max. take-off, 13,889 lb (6 300 kg); max. payload, 4,409 lb (2 000 kg).
Accommodation: Flight crew of two and 18 passengers in commercial configuration. Ten casualty stretchers and three sitting casualties as ambulance. Provision for up to 15 paratroops and jumpmaster or 4,409 lb (2 000 kg) of cargo.
Status: Two prototypes flown March 26 and October 23, 1971, with first of 12 pre-production examples following November 17, 1972. Initial production batch of 32 for Spanish Air Force with deliveries commencing early 1974.
Notes: Of pre-production series, eight have been delivered to Air Force (six for photo survey as C.212Bs and two as C.212E navigational trainers), and the initial production batch has been delivered as C.212A utility transports. Current orders include 22 C.212As and two C.212Bs for Portugal, four C.212As for Jordan and 16 C.212As and commercial C.212Cs for Indonesia.

CASA C.212 AVIOCAR

Dimensions: Span, 62 ft 4 in (19,00 m); length, 49 ft 10½ in (15,20 m); height, 20 ft 8¾ in (6,32 m); wing area, 430·556 sq ft (40,0 m²).

CESSNA 404 TITAN

Country of Origin: USA.

Type: Light business executive transport and third-level airliner.

Power Plant: Two 375 hp Teledyne Continental GTSIO-520X six-cylinder horizontally-opposed engines.

Performance: Max. speed, 225 mph (363 km/h) at sea level, 269 mph (433 km/h) at 16,000 ft (4 877 m); max. cruise (75% power), 223 mph (359 km/h) at 10,000 ft (3 048 m), 246 mph (396 km/h) at 20,000 ft (6 096 m); range (with 10 occupants), 1,020 mls (1 641 km) at 221 mph (356 km/h) at 10,000 ft (3 048 m); initial climb, 1,515 ft/min (7,69 m/sec); service ceiling, 22,200 ft (6 767 m).

Weights: Empty (Ambassador), 4,754 lb (2 156 kg), (Courier), 4,773 lb (2 165 kg); max. take-off, 8,300 lb (3 765 kg).

Accommodation: Two seats side by side in cockpit and maximum of eight individual seats in pairs in main cabin.

Status: Prototype flown on February 26, 1975, and customer deliveries scheduled to commence mid-1976, current production planning calling for an output of 12 Titans monthly.

Notes: The Titan is to be offered in two versions: the Courier commuter and freight transport and the Ambassador business executive transport with customised interior arrangement. Utilising the same primary airframe as the turboprop-powered Model 441 (see pages 60–61), the Titan includes bonded structures in its wings and features large hydraulic Fowler flaps, advanced-design propellers and trailing-link main undercarriage members to provide good capability for operation from short, rough strips.

CESSNA 404 TITAN

Dimensions: Span, 46 ft 0 in (14,02 m); length, 39 ft 6 in (12,04 m); height, 13 ft 1 in (3,99 m); wing area, 242 sq ft (22,48 m²).

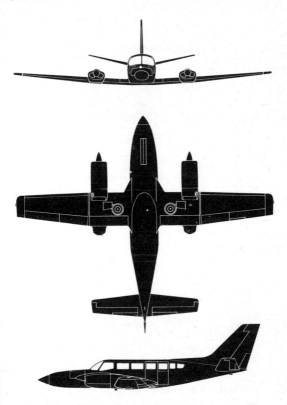

CESSNA 441

Country of Origin: USA.

Type: Light business executive aircraft.

Power Plant: Two 620 shp Garrett-AiResearch TPE-331-8-401 turboprops.

Performance: Max. speed, 325 mph (523 km/h) at 16,000 ft (4 877 m); max. cruise, 322 mph (519 km/h) at 17,000 ft (5 182 m); range at max. cruise with 45 min reserves (10 occupants), 1,335 mls (2 148 km) at 33,000 ft (10 058 m), 869 mls (1 398 km) at 17,000 ft (5 182 m), (five occupants), 2,106 mls (3 389 km) at 33,000 ft (10 058 m), 1,335 mls (2 148 km) at 17,000 ft (5 182 m); initial climb, 2,405 ft/min (12,2 m/sec); service ceiling, 33,200 ft (10 120 m).

Weights: Empty, 5,045 lb (2 288 kg); max. take-off, 9,500 lb (4 309 kg).

Accommodation: Two seats side by side in cockpit and maximum of eight individual seats in pairs in main cabin.

Status: Prototype flown on August 26, 1975, with initial customer deliveries scheduled for late 1977 as part of the Cessna 1978 Model range. Tooling is in preparation for the production of 15 Model 441s per month.

Notes: Intended to fit into the market between existing piston-engined twins and turbofan-powered business aircraft, the Model 441 is Cessna's first turboprop-powered type to attain production status.

CESSNA 441

Dimensions: Span, 46 ft 4 in (14,12 m); length, 39 ft $0\frac{1}{4}$ in (11,89 m); height, 13ft 1 in (3,99 m); wing area, 242 sq ft (22,48 m²).

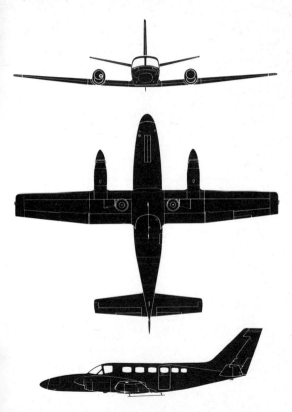

CESSNA CITATION SERIES 500

Country of Origin: USA.

Type: Light business executive transport.

Power Plant: Two 2,200 lb (1 000 kg) Pratt & Whitney (Canada) JT15D-1 turbofans.

Performance: Max. speed, 402 mph (647 km/h) at 26,400 ft (8 046 m); max. cruise, 400 mph (644 km/h) at 25,400 ft (7 740 m); range with eight persons and 45 min reserves at 90% cruise thrust, 1,397 mls (2 248 km), with two persons and same reserves at 90% cruise thrust, 1,502 mls (2 417 km); initial climb, 2,900 ft/min (14,7 m/sec); service ceiling, 38,400 ft (11 704 m).

Weights: Empty, 6,454 lb (2 927 kg); max. take-off, 11,850 lb (5 375 kg).

Accommodation: Crew of two on separate flight deck and alternative arrangements for five or six passengers in main cabin.

Status: First of two prototypes flown on September 15, 1969, and first production Citation flown in May 1971. Customer deliveries began in October 1971. Deliveries averaged six per month during 1974, and approximately 300 had been delivered by the beginning of 1976.

Notes: The Citation places emphasis on short-field performance, enabling the aircraft to use some 2,300 US airfields. From early 1975, operational ceiling was increased from 35,000 to 41,000 ft (10 670 to 12 495 m) and with the 275th aircraft a lighter-weight avionics package and an increase in max. take-off weight permits a 1,400-mile (2 253-km) VFR range with six passengers and full fuel.

CESSNA CITATION SERIES 500

Dimensions: Span, 43 ft 11 in (13,39 m); length, 43 ft 6 in (13,26 m); height, 14 ft 3¾ in (4,36 m); wing area, 260 sq ft (24,15 m²).

DASSAULT-BREGUET FALCON 10

Country of Origin: France.

Type: Light business executive transport.

Power Plant: Two 3,230 lb (1 465 kg) Garrett-AiResearch TFE-731-2 turbofans.

Performance: Max. cruise, 567 mph (912 km/h) at 30,000 ft (9 145 m), 495 mph (796 km/h) or Mach 0·75 at 45,000 ft (13 716 m); range with four passengers and 45 min reserves, 2,070 mls (3 330 km) at 45,000 ft (13 716 m), 1,495 mls (2 405 km) at max. cruise at 30,000 ft (9 145 m).

Weights: Empty equipped, 10,760 lb (4 880 kg); max. take-off, 18,740 lb (8 500 kg).

Accommodation: Flight crew of two with provision for third crew member on jump seat. Executive version for four passengers with alternative arrangement for seven passengers.

Status: First of three prototypes flown December 1, 1970, followed by second on October 15, 1971, and third on October 16, 1972. The first production Falcon 10 was flown on April 30, 1973, and production deliveries began during November of that year, output being two per month at the beginning of 1976 when some 50 aircraft had been delivered.

Notes: The Falcon 10 (also known as the Mystère 10) is basically a scaled-down version of the Falcon 20 (see 1974 edition), and at a later stage in development it is proposed to offer the 2,980 lb (1 350 kg) Turboméca-SNECMA Larzac turbofan as an alternative power plant. The Falcon 10 is being offered to the *Armée de l'Air* as a military crew trainer and liaison aircraft, and two examples have been delivered to France's *Aéronavale* (which has an option on three more) primarily for radar training under the designation Falcon 10 MER.

DASSAULT-BREGUET FALCON 10

Dimensions: 42 ft 11 in (13,08 m); length, 45 ft 5¾ in (13,86 m); height, 15 ft 1 in (4,61 m); wing area, 259·4 sq ft 24,1 m²).

DASSAULT-BREGUET FALCON 50

Country of Origin: France.

Type: Light business executive transport.

Power Plant: Three 3,700 lb (1 680 kg) Garrett AiResearch TFE 731-3 turbofans.

Performance: (Estimated) Max. operating speed, 560 mph (900 km/h) at 36,090 ft (11 000 m) or Mach 0·85; max. cruise, 540 mph (840 km/h) or Mach 0·81; econ. cruise, 472–490 mph (760–790 km/h); range (four passengers and VFR reserves), 3,625 mls (5 830 km), (six passengers and IFR reserves), 3,090 mls (4 970 km).

Weights: Empty equipped, 19,845 lb (9 000 kg); max. take-off, 36,600 lb (16 600 kg).

Accommodation: Flight crew of two and 6–10 passengers.

Status: Prototype scheduled to fly November 1976, with first customer delivery (No 4 aircraft) July–August 1978.

Notes: Since the Falcon 50 was first announced (see 1975 edition) it has undergone considerable redesign, the principal new features visible externally being a thicker wing of greater span and reduced sweepback and the use of seven rather than six windows in each side of the fuselage. Originally it was intended that the Falcon 50 would employ the basic fuselage, wing and horizontal tail of the Falcon 20 Series F (see 1974 edition), and the decision to undertake major redesign has imposed a one-year delay in the projected schedule for Falcon 50 deliveries. A production rate of three Falcon 50s per month is planned to be achieved by mid-1979 with the 25th aircraft being delivered by the end of that year.

DASSAULT-BREGUET FALCON 50

Dimensions: Span, 61 ft 10 in (18,85 m); length, 60 ft 0½ in (18,30 m); height, 18 ft 8 in (5,70 m); wing area, 495 sq ft (46,0 m²).

DASSAULT-BREGUET MIRAGE 50

Country of Origin: France.

Type: Single-seat multi-role fighter.

Power Plant: One 11,023 lb (5 000 kg) dry and 15,873 lb (7 200 kg) reheat SNECMA Atar 9K-50 turbojet.

Performance: Max. speed (clean), 835 mph (1 335 km/h) or Mach 1·1 at sea level, 1,450 mph (2 335 km/h) or Mach 2·2 at 39,370 ft (12 000 m); approx. combat radius with 2,000-lb (907-kg) external weapons load (hi-lo-hi), 850 mls (1 370 km), (lo-lo-lo), 420 mls (675 km); time to reach Mach 1·8 at 39,370 ft (12 000 m) with two Magic AAMs, 4·4min.

Weights: Empty equipped, 15,875 lb (7 200 kg); loaded (clean), 21,830 lb (9 900 kg); max. take-off, 30,210 lb (13 700 kg).

Armament: Two 30-mm DEFA 5-52 cannon with 125 rpg and max. external load of ordnance and fuel on seven external stations of 9,260 lb (4 200 kg).

Status: Prototype Mirage 50—employing the Mirage IIIE airframe previously utilised as the Milan (Kite) test aircraft—flown 1974, with fully representative prototype under construction for test and demonstration during course of 1976.

Notes: The Mirage 50 is essentially a Mirage 5 airframe (see 1975 edition) mated with the Atar 9K-50 turbojet employed by the Mirage F1, with new avionics and improvements in the overall weapons system. The Atar 9K-50 affords a substantial increase in thrust (16% for take-off with reheat and 10% at Mach 2·0 at 36,090 ft/11 000 m) and lower specific fuel consumption by comparison with the Atar 9C of the Mirage 5, resulting in reduced take-off run (up to 22% at max. weight) and a 30% improvement in initial climb rate. Modified air intakes cater for the higher mass flow and the undercarriage is strengthened.

DASSAULT-BREGUET MIRAGE 50

Dimensions: Span, 26 ft 11½ in (8,22 m); length, 51 ft 0¼ in (15,55 m); height, 14 ft 9 in (4,50 m); wing area, ˙375·12 sq ft (34,85 m²).

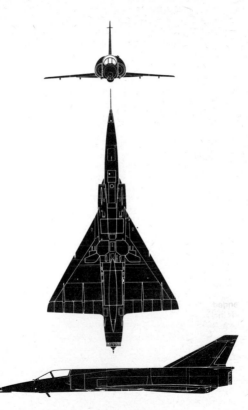

DASSAULT-BREGUET MIRAGE F1

Country of Origin: France.
Type: Single-seat multi-purpose fighter.
Power Plant: One 11,023 lb (5 000 kg) dry and 15,873 lb (7 200 kg) reheat SNECMA Atar 9K-50 turbojet.
Performance: Max. speed (clean), 915 mph (1 472 km/h) or Mach 1·2 at sea level, 1,450 mph (2 335 km/h) or Mach 2·2 at 39,370 ft (12 000 m); range cruise, 550 mph (885 km/h) at 29,530 ft (9 000 m); range with max. external fuel, 2,050 mls (3 300 km), with max. external combat load of 8,818 lb (4 000 kg), 560 mls (900 km), with external combat load of 4,410 lb (2 000 kg), 1,430 mls (2 300 km); service ceiling, 65,600 ft (20 000 m).
Weights: Empty, 16,314 lb (7 400 kg); loaded (clean), 24,030 lb (10 900 kg); max. take-off, 32,850 lb (14 900 kg).
Armament: Two 30-mm DEFA cannon and (intercept) 1-3 Matra 530 Magic and two AIM-9 Sidewinder AAMs.
Status: First of four prototypes flown December 23, 1966. First of 105 ordered for *Armée de l'Air* flown February 15, 1973. Production rate of four–five per month at beginning of 1976. Licence manufacture is to be undertaken in South Africa with deliveries commencing 1977.
Notes: Initial model for *Armée de l'Air* intended primarily for high-altitude intercept role. Proposed versions include F1A and F1E for the ground attack role, the F1B and F1D two-seat trainers and the F1C interceptor. Fifteen Mirage F1Cs have been ordered by Spain (which country has an option on 18 more), 40 by Greece and 20 by Kuwait; delivery of 16 Mirage F1CZ interceptors to South Africa began late 1974, these being followed by 32 Mirage F1AZ ground attack fighters, and 38 (32 Mirage F1As and F1Es and six two-seat F1Bs and F1Ds) have been ordered by Libya.

DASSAULT-BREGUET MIRAGE F1

Dimensions: Span, 27 ft 6¾ in (8,40 m); length, 49 ft 2½ in (15,00 m); height, 14 ft 9 in (4,50 m); wing area, 269·098 sq ft (25 m²).

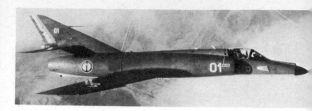

DASSAULT-BREGUET SUPER ÉTENDARD

Country of Origin: France.

Type: Single-seat shipboard strike fighter.

Power Plant: One 11,025 lb (5 000 kg) SNECMA Atar 8K-50 turbojet.

Performance: Max. speed, 745 mph (1 200 km/h) at 985 ft (300 m) or Mach 0·97, 695 mph (1 118 km/h) at 36,000 ft (11 000 m) or Mach 1·05; radius of action (hi-lo-hi with 2,200-lb/998-kg bomb load), 225 mls (360 km), (lo-lo-lo), 160 mls (260 km), (anti-shipping mission with AM-39 Exocet ASM and 1,700-lb/771-kg bomb load), 255 mls (410 km).

Weights: Empty, 13,780 lb (6 250 kg); max. take-off (catapult), 25,350 lb (11 500 kg); overload, 26,455 lb (12 000 kg).

Armament: Two 30-mm DEFA 552A cannon with 122 rpg and a variety of ordnance on five external stores stations (four wing and one fuselage), including Matra 550 Magic AAMs, AM-39 Exocet ASM, etc.

Status: First of three Super Étendard development aircraft (converted from Étendard airframes) flown on October 28, 1974, the second and third flying on March 28 and March 9, 1975, respectively. First production aircraft built against initial contract for 30 scheduled for delivery in March 1977. Anticipated production rate of two per month. Total *Aéronavale* requirement for 80–100 aircraft.

Notes: The Super Étendard is a more powerful derivative of the Étendard IVM (see 1965 edition) with new avionics, a revised wing and other changes. The Super Étendard is intended to serve aboard the carriers Clémenceau and Foch.

72

DASSULT-BREGUET SUPER ÉTENDARD

Dimensions: Span, 31 ft 6 in (9,60 m); length, 46 ft 11½ in (14,31 m); height, 12 ft 8 in (3,85 m); wing area, 305·7 sq ft (28,40 m²).

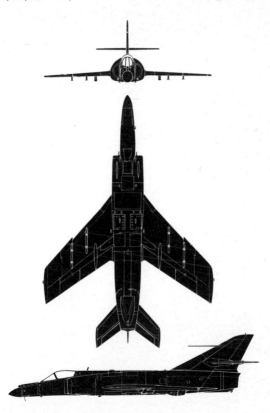

DASSAULT-BREGUET/DORNIER
ALPHA JET

Countries of Origin: France and Federal Germany.
Type: Two-seat advanced trainer and light tactical aircraft.
Power Plant: Two 2,975 lb (1 350 kg) SNECMA-Turbo-méca Larzac 04 turbofans.
Performance: Max. speed, 626 mph (991 km/h) at sea level, 560 mph (901 km/h) at 40,000 ft (12 190 m) or Mach 0·85; radius of action (hi-lo-hi), 390 mls (630 km); max. fuel endurance, 2 hrs at sea level, 3 hrs at 32,810 ft (10 000 m); ferry range (max. external fuel), 1,900 mls (3 057 km); initial climb, 11,800 ft/min (59 m/sec); service ceiling, 45,000 ft (13 700 m).
Weights: Empty equipped, 6,944 lb (3 150 kg); operational empty, 7,661 lb (3 475 kg); normal take-off (trainer), 10,780 lb (4 890 kg), (close support), 13,227 lb (6 000 kg); max. overload, 15,340 lb (7 000 kg).
Armament: Provision for external gun pod with 30-mm DEFA 533 cannon or 27-mm Mauser cannon and 150 rounds. Close support version has four wing strong points, inboard points being stressed for loads up to 1,250 lb (570 kg) each and outboard points for loads up to 630 lb (285 kg) each. Maximum external load is 4,850 lb (2 200 kg).
Status: First of four prototypes flown on October 26, 1973, with last flying on October 11, 1974. Planned production of approx. 200 each for *Armée de l'Air* and *Luftwaffe* with deliveries commencing during course of 1977. Thirty-three to be supplied to Belgium with deliveries commencing November 1978.
Notes: The Alpha Jet is to have two final assembly lines (Toulouse and Munich) and will serve with the *Armée de l'Air* in the training role and for close support with the *Luftwaffe*.

DASSAULT-BREGUET/DORNIER ALPHA JET

Dimensions: Span, 29 ft 11 in (9,11 m); length, 40 ft 3 in (12,29 m); height, 13 ft 9 in (4,19 m); wing area, 188 sq ft (17,50 m²).

DE HAVILLAND CANADA DHC-6
TWIN OTTER SERIES 300

Country of Origin: Canada.
Type: STOL utility transport and feederliner.
Power Plant: Two 652 eshp UACL PT6A-27 turboprops.
Performance: Max. cruise, 210 mph (338 km/h) at 10,000 ft (3 050 m); range at max. cruise with 3,250-lb (1 474-kg) payload, 745 mls (1 198 km), with 14 passengers and 45 min reserves, 780 mls (1 255 km); initial climb at 12,500 lb (5 670 kg), 1,600 ft/min (8,1 m/sec); service ceiling, 26,700 ft (8 138 m).
Weights: Basic operational (including pilot), 7,000 lb (3 180 kg); max. take-off, 12,500 lb (5 670 kg).
Accommodation: Flight crew of one or two and accommodation for up to 20 passengers in basic commuter arrangement. Optional commuter layouts for 18 or 19 passengers, and 13–20-passenger utility version.
Status: First of five (Series 100) pre-production aircraft flown May 20, 1965. Series 100 superseded by Series 200 (see 1969 edition) in April 1968, the latter being joined by the Series 300 with the 231st aircraft off the assembly line, deliveries of this version commencing spring 1969. Total ordered by beginning of 1976 in excess of 500.
Notes: Series 100 and 200 Twin Otters feature a shorter nose and have 579 eshp PT6A-20s, and the Twin Otter is available as a floatplane. The Series 300S introduced in 1973 featured upper wing spoilers, high-capacity brakes, an anti-skid braking system and other improvements to suit it for use with the Canadian Government's Montreal–Ottawa intercity STOL demonstration system.

DHC-6 TWIN OTTER SERIES 300

Dimensions: Span, 65 ft 0 in (19,81 m); length, 51 ft 9 in (15,77 m); height, 18 ft 7 in (5,66 m); wing area, 420 sq ft (39,02 m²).

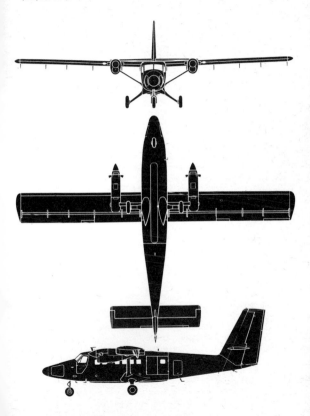

DE HAVILLAND CANADA DHC-7 DASH-7

Country of Origin: Canada.

Type: STOL short-haul commercial transport.

Power Plant: Four 1,120 shp Pratt & Whitney (Canada) PT6A-50 turboprops.

Performance: Max. cruise, 281 mph (452 km/h) at 15,000 ft (4 570 m); long-range cruise, 259 mph (416 km/h) at 20,000 ft (6 560 m); range (at 80% max. cruise with max. passenger payload and reserves), 935 mls (1 504 km); max. range (with 7,080-lb/3 211-kg payload at 80% max. cruise), 1,425 mls (2 293 km).

Weights: Operational empty, 25,860 lb (11 730 kg); max. take-off, 43,000 lb (19 504 kg).

Accommodation: Flight crew of two and standard seating for 50 passengers in pairs on each side of central aisle.

Status: First of two pre-production aircraft flown on March 27, 1975, with second following on June 26, 1975. First customer deliveries scheduled to commence spring 1977, with production tempo of four per month planned by 1978. Total of 33 ordered by beginning of 1976.

Notes: The Dash-7 STOL (Short Take-Off and Landing) transport is being funded by de Havilland Canada, United Technologies Corporation (manufacturer of the engines) and the Canadian Government, and is the result of a worldwide market survey of short-haul transport requirements. The Dash-7 can operate from 2,000-ft (610-m) runways with a full passenger load and features a quiet engine/propeller combination which limits external noise during take-off and landing. Certification of the Dash-7 is scheduled for late 1976.

DE HAVILLAND CANADA DHC-7 DASH-7

Dimensions: Span, 93 ft 0 in (28,35 m); length, 80 ft 7¾ in (24,58 m); height, 26 ft 2 in (7,98 m); wing area, 860 sq ft (79,9 m²).

DOMINION SKYTRADER 800

Country of Origin: USA.
Type: Light STOL utility transport.
Power Plant: Two 400 hp Avco Lycoming IO-720-B1A eight-cylinder horizontally-opposed engines.
Performance: Max. speed, 210 mph (338 km/h); max. cruise (75% power), 170 mph (274 km/h) at 10,000 ft (3 050 m); cruise (55% power), 150 mph (241 km/h) at 2,500 ft (762 m); max. range (75% power), 930 mls (1 495 km), (55% power), 1,430 mls (2 300 km), (with auxiliary external tanks at 55% power), 2,450 mls (3 940 km); max. initial climb, 1,600 ft/min (8,10 m/sec); service ceiling, 17,500 ft (5 338 m).
Weights: Empty, 5,450 lb (2 474 kg); max. take-off, 9,000 lb (4 086 kg).
Accommodation: Pilot and co-pilot/passenger at front of cabin with various internal arrangements including 12 passengers in individual seats, a six-seat executive layout or all-freight configuration.
Status: Prototype flown on April 21, 1975. Deliveries of production model scheduled to commence spring 1976 with an initial batch of 60 being laid down for production at five per month.
Notes: The Skytrader was originally intended for manufacture in Canada, but owing to the Dominion Aircraft Corporation's inability to establish suitable financing arrangements, production is being undertaken at Renton, Washington. The Skytrader has been designed primarily as a "bush" transport and is stressed for engines up to 650 hp.

DOMINION SKYTRADER 800

Dimensions: Span, 55 ft 0 in (16,76 m); length, 42 ft 0 in (12,81 m); height, 18 ft 10¾ in (5,76 m); wing area, 385 sq ft (35,77 m²).

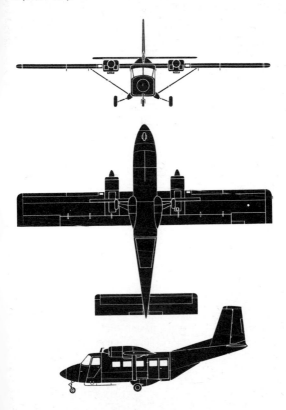

EMBRAER EMB-121 XINGU

Country of Origin: Brazil.

Type: Light business executive transport.

Power Plant: Two 680 shp Pratt & Whitney (Canada) PT6A-28 turboprops.

Performance: Max. cruise, 292 mph (470 km/h) at 15,000 ft (4 575 m); econ. cruise, 280 mph (450 km/h); range (with six passengers and 45 min reserves), 1,430 mls (2 300 km).

Weights: Empty equipped, 6,892 lb (3 126 kg); max. take-off, 11,464 lb (5 200 kg).

Accommodation: Two seats side-by-side on flight deck and six to seven passengers in individual seats in main cabin.

Status: The first prototype Xingu was scheduled to commence its flight test programme in January 1976, with proposed customer deliveries commencing late 1977.

Notes: The Xingu is the first of the EMB-12X series of pressurised light transports evolved from the EMB-110 Bandeirante (see 1975 edition), further developments being the 10-passenger EMB-123 Tapajós and the 20-passenger EMB-120 Araguaia. By comparison with the Bandeirante, the Xingu has a shorter, pressurised fuselage, but both the Tapajós and Araguaia will feature a supercritical wing and will be powered by 1,120 shp PT6A-45 turboprops. Both will have an essentially similar fuselage to that of the Xingu, the fuselage length of the Tapajós being stretched to 46 ft 11 in (13,30 m) and that of the Araguaia to 52 ft 11 in (16,13 m). Both the Tapajós and the Araguaia are expected to commence their flight test programmes during the course of 1977.

EMBRAER EMB-121 XINGU

Dimensions: Span, 45 ft 11$\frac{7}{8}$ in (14,02 m); length, 41 ft 0$\frac{9}{10}$ in (12,52 m); height, 15 ft 5$\frac{4}{5}$ in (4,72 m).

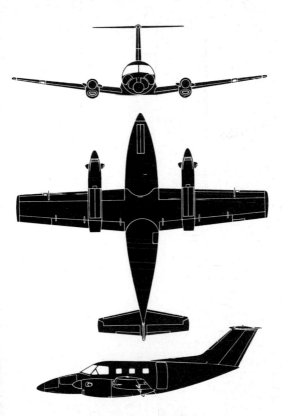

FAIRCHILD A-10A

Country of Origin: USA.

Type: Single-seat close-support aircraft.

Power Plant: Two 9,065 lb (4 112 kg) General Electric TF34-GE-100 turbofans.

Performance: Max. speed (clean), 449 mph (722 km/h) at sea level, (with six Mk. 82 bombs), 453 mph (729 km/h) at 5,000 ft (1 525 m); cruise, 345 mph (555 km/h) at sea level; operational radius (deep strike), 620 mls (1 000 km), (reconnaissance), 499 mls (803 km); (close air support with 2·2 hrs loiter and 20 min reserves), 288 mls (463 km); ferry range, 2,888 mls (4 647 km); max. initial climb (at 30,044 lb/13 628 kg), 6,000 ft/min (30,48 m/sec).

Weights: Empty, 20,231 lb (9 176 kg); max. take-off, 46,624 lb (21 148 kg).

Armament: One 30-mm General Electric GAU-8/A seven-barrel rotary cannon with 1,350 rounds and max. external ordnance load of 16,000 lb (7 257 kg) on 11 external stores stations (eight under wings and three under fuselage). Typical external payload of 9,540 lb (4 327 kg) with 2,200 lb (998 kg) ammunition internally and 10,650 lb (4 831 kg) of fuel.

Status: First of two prototypes flown May 10, 1972, and first of six pre-production aircraft February 15, 1975. Initial contracts for 52 production A-10As against anticipated requirement for 700 plus, the first of these aircraft having flown on October 21, 1975. First USAF A-10A squadron was to form February 1976.

Notes: The A-10A was announced winning contender in the USAF's A-X close-support aircraft contest on January 18, 1973.

FAIRCHILD A-10A

Dimensions: Span, 57 ft 6 in (17,53 m); length, 53 ft 4 in (16,26 m); height, 14 ft 8 in (4,47 m); wing area, 506 sq ft (47,01 m²).

FOKKER F.27 FRIENDSHIP SRS. 500

Country of Origin: Netherlands.

Type: Short- to medium-range commercial transport.

Power Plant: Two 2,250 eshp Rolls-Royce Dart 532-7 turboprops.

Performance: Max. cruise, 322 mph (518 km/h) at 20,000 ft (6 095 m); normal cruise at 38,000 lb (17 237 kg), 298 mph (480 km/h) at 20,000 ft (6 095 m); range with max. payload, 667 mls (1 075 km), with max. fuel and 9,680-lb (4 390-kg) payload, 1,099 mls (1 805 km); initial climb at max. take-off weight, 1,200 ft/min (6,1 m/sec); service ceiling at 38,000 lb (17 237 kg), 29,500 ft (9 000 m).

Weights: Empty, 24,886 lb (11 288 kg); operational empty, 25,951 lb (11 771 kg); max. take-off, 45,000 lb (20 411 kg).

Accommodation: Basic flight crew of two or three and standard seating for 52 passengers. Alternative arrangements for up to 56 passengers.

Status: First Srs. 500 flown November 15, 1967. Production currently standardising on Srs. 500 and 600. Orders for the Friendship (including 205 licence-built in the USA by Fairchild) totalled 648 by beginning of 1976 when production rate was two per month.

Notes: By comparison with basic Srs. 200 (see 1968 edition), the Srs. 500 has a 4 ft 11 in (1,5 m) fuselage stretch. The Srs. 400 ''Combiplane'' (see 1966 edition) and the equivalent military Srs. 400M (illustrated above) are convertible cargo or combined cargo-passenger versions of the Srs. 200, and the current Srs. 600 is similar to the Srs. 400 but lacks the reinforced and watertight cargo floor.

FOKKER F.27 FRIENDSHIP SRS. 500

Dimensions: Span, 95 ft $1\frac{3}{4}$ in (29,00 m); length, 82 ft $2\frac{1}{2}$ in (25,06 m); height, 28 ft $7\frac{1}{4}$ in (8,71 m); wing area, 753·47 sq ft (70 m²).

FOKKER F.28 FELLOWSHIP MK. 6000

Country of Origin: Netherlands.

Type: Short-haul commercial transport.

Power Plant: Two 9,850 lb (4 468 kg) Rolls-Royce RB.183-2 Spey Mk. 555-15H turbofans.

Performance: Max. cruise, 523 mph (843 km/h) at 23,000 ft (7 000 m); econ. cruise, 421 mph (678 km/h) at 30,000 ft (9 150 m); range (high-speed schedule), 1,036 mls (1 667 km), (long-range schedule), 1,185 mls (1 908 km); max. cruise altitude, 35,000 ft (10 675 m).

Weights: Operational empty, 38,345 lb (17 393 kg); max. take-off, 70,800 lb (32 115 kg).

Accommodation: Flight crew of two or three. Main cabin layout may be varied to accommodate 55, 60, 65 or 79 passengers in five-abreast seating.

Status: The prototype Fellowship Mk. 6000 (the fuselage of the prototype Mk. 2000 and the modified wings of the second Mk. 1000 prototype) flew September 27, 1973. First production aircraft obtained Certificate of Airworthiness on November 5, 1975, when production of all versions of the Fellowship was running at two per month. A total of 107 Fellowships had been ordered by the beginning of 1976.

Notes: The Fellowship Mk. 6000 is a derivative of the stretched-fuselage Mk. 2000, offering improved field performance and payload/range capabilities. Wing span is increased by 4 ft 11½ in (1,50 m), three-section leading-edge slats have been added to each wing and an improved version of the Spey engine has been adopted. Similar changes to the basic (shorter-fuselage) Fellowship Mk. 1000 will result in the Mk. 5000 which will be available with large cargo door.

FOKKER F.28 FELLOWSHIP MK. 6000

Dimensions: Span, 82 ft 3 in (25,07 m); length, 97 ft 1¾ in (29,61 m); height, 27 ft 9½ in (8,47 m); wing area, 850 sq ft (78,97 m²).

FUJI KM-2B

Country of Origin: Japan.

Type: Tandem two-seat primary trainer.

Power Plant: One 340 hp Avco Lycoming IGSO-480-A1A6 six-cylinder horizontally-opposed engine.

Performance: Max. speed, 234 mph (376 km/h) at 16,000 ft (4 877 m); max. cruise, 204 mph (328 km/h) at 8,000 ft (2 438 m); econ. cruise, 158 (254 km/h) at 8,000 ft (2 438 m); max. range, 645 mls (1 037 km); max. climb rate, 1,520 ft/min (7,62 m/sec); service ceiling, 26,800 ft (8 170 m).

Weights: Empty, 2,470 lb (1 120 kg); max. take-off, 3,330 lb (1 510 kg).

Status: Prototype flown on September 26, 1974, with production of an initial batch of 12 aircraft scheduled to commence during 1976 against planned Air Self-Defence Force procurement of 60 aircraft.

Notes: The KM-2B is the result of two decades of Japanese development of the Beechcraft B45 Mentor, licence manufacture of 126 examples of which was undertaken by Fuji after assembly of 50 from components supplied by the parent manufacturer. A Fuji-developed side-by-side two-seat derivative of the Mentor, the LM-1, was flown in July 1955, 27 being built for the Ground Self-Defence Force, a more powerful development, the KM Super Nikko, following in December 1958. The Super Nikko was subsequently adopted by the Maritime Self-Defence Force as the KM-2 side-by-side basic trainer and the KM-2B is an updated, tandem-seat development.

FUJI KM-2B

Dimensions: Span, 32 ft 9⅞ in (10,00 m); length, 26 ft 4½ in (8,04 m); height, 9 ft 10⅞ in (3,02 m); wing area, 177·6 sq ft (16,50 m²).

GAF NOMAD

Country of Origin: Australia.

Type: STOL military and commercial utility transport.

Power Plant: Two 400 shp Allison 250-B17B turboprops.

Performance: (N22B) Max. cruise, 193 mph (311 km/h) at sea level, 196 mph (315 km/h) at 5,000 ft (1 525 m); long-range cruise, 167 mph (269 km/h); range with 45 min reserves, 58 mls (93 km) with 3,400-lb (1 543-kg) payload, 990 mls (1 593 km) with 1,717-lb (779-kg) payload; initial climb, 1,410 ft/min (7,16 m/sec); service ceiling, 22,500 ft (6 858 m).

Weights: (N22B) Operational empty, 4,670 lb (2 120 kg); max. take-off, 8,500 lb (3 865 kg).

Accommodation: Flight crew of one or two and individual seats for up to 12 passengers.

Status: First and second prototypes of Nomad 22 flown July 23 and December 5, 1971, respectively, and first production aircraft flown May 1975. First stretched N24 flown July 1975, and first commercial delivery (N22B) September 1975. Production tempo was being increased from three to four per month at beginning of 1976 when total orders (both N22 and N24) exceeded 60 aircraft.

Notes: Current Nomad production includes the military N22 Mission Master ordered for the Australian Army, the Indonesian Navy, the Peruvian Army and the Philippine Air Force, the commercial N22B, the first export delivery of which was to Sabah Air, and the stretched N24 which has a 43-in (1,09-m) additional cabin section.

GAF NOMAD

Dimensions: Span, 54 ft 0 in (16,46 m); length, 41 ft 2½ in (12,57 m); height, 18 ft 1½ in (5,52 m); wing area, 324 sq ft (30,10 m²).

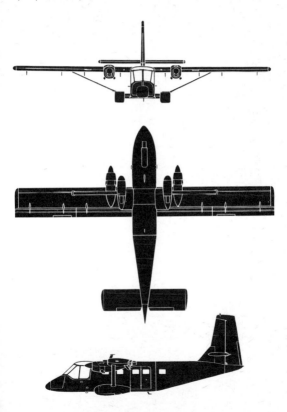

GATES LEARJET 35A

Country of Origin: USA.

Type: Light business executive transport.

Power Plant: Two 3,500 lb (1 588 kg) Garrett AiResearch TFE 731-2 turbofans.

Performance: Max. speed, 565 mph (910 km/h) or Mach 0·83; max. cruise, 534 mph (859 km/h); normal cruise, 507 mph (816 km/h); range (with four passengers and 45 min reserves), 2,858 mls (4 600 km); initial climb, 5,100 ft/min (25·9 m/sec); time to 41,000 ft (12 500 m), 18 min.

Weights: Empty equipped, 8,802 lb (3 992 kg); max. take-off, 17,000 lb (7 711 kg).

Accommodation: Two pilots or pilot and passenger on flight deck and up to seven passengers in main cabin.

Status: Prototype Learjet 35 flown on August 22, 1973, with first customer delivery in November 1974. To be succeeded by Learjet 35A from summer of 1976 as one of the so-called Century III series of Learjets.

Notes: The Century III series of Learjets announced October 28, 1975, for mid-1976 delivery feature a modified aerofoil and other aerodynamic improvements. Six models are available: the Learjet 24E and 24F with General Electric CJ610-6 turbojets of 2,950 lb (1 340 kg), the similarly-powered Learjet 25D and 25F embodying a 4 ft 2 in (1,27 m) fuselage stretch, and the Learjet 35A and 36A with turbofans and marginally enlarged overall dimensions (by comparison with the 25D and 25F). By comparison with the 35A, the Learjet 36A has increased fuel capacity resulting in a range of 3,410 miles (5 488 km) with four passengers and reserves.

GATES LEARJET 35A

Dimensions: Span, 39 ft 8 in (12,09 m); length, 48 ft 8 in (14,83 m); height, 12 ft 3 in (3,73 m); wing area, 253·3 sq ft (23,5 m²).

GENERAL DYNAMICS F-16

Country of Origin: USA.

Type: Single-seat air combat fighter (F-16A) and two-seat operational trainer (F-16B).

Power Plant: One (approx.) 25,000 lb (11 340 kg) reheat Pratt & Whitney F100-PW-100(3) turbofan.

Performance: Max. speed (with two Sidewinder AAMs), 1,255 mph (2 020 km/h) at 36,000 ft (10 970 m) or Mach 1·95, 915 mph (1 472 km/h) at sea level or Mach 1·2; tactical radius (interdiction mission hi-lo-hi on internal fuel with six Mk. 82 bombs), 340 mls (550 km); ferry range, 2,300+ mls (3 700+ km); initial climb, 62,000 ft/min (315 m/sec); service ceiling, 52,000 ft (15 850 m).

Weights: Operational empty, 14,100 lb (6 395 kg); loaded (full internal fuel), 22,200 lb (10 070 kg); max. take-off, 33,000 lb (14 969 kg).

Armament: One 20-mm M-61A-1 Vulcan rotary cannon with 500 rounds and up to 11,000 lb (4 990 kg) of stores on nine external (two wingtip, six underwing and one fuselage) stores stations, or 15,200 lb (6 894 kg) with reduced internal fuel.

Status: First of two (YF-16) prototypes flown on January 20, 1974. First of eight pre-production aircraft (six single-seat F-16As and two two-seat F-16Bs) scheduled to fly during last quarter of 1976. Planned USAF procurement of 650 aircraft. Total of 348 on order or option for four European NATO countries as follows: Netherlands (84 plus 18 on option), Belgium (102 plus 14 on option), Denmark (48 plus 10 on option) and Norway (72). First production F-16A for USAF scheduled to be completed August 1978.

Notes: YF-16 selected in preference to Northrop YF-17 (see 1975 edition) to meet USAF's ACF (Air Combat Fighter) requirement.

GENERAL DYNAMICS F-16

Dimensions: Span (excluding missiles), 31 ft 0 in (9,45 m);
length, 47 ft 7¾ in (14,52 m); height, 16 ft 5¼ in (5,01 m);
wing area, 300 sq ft (27,87 m²).

GRUMMAN A-6E INTRUDER

Country of Origin: USA.

Type: Two-seat shipboard low-level strike aircraft.

Power Plant: Two 9,300 lb (4 218 kg) Pratt & Whitney J52-P-8A/B turbojets.

Performance: Max. speed (clean), 654 mph (1 052 km/h) at sea level or Mach 0·86, 625 mph (1 006 km/h) at 36,000 ft (10 970 m) or Mach 0·94, (close support role with 28 Mk. 81 Snakeye bombs), 557 mph (896 km/h) at 5,000 ft (1 525 m); combat range (clean), 2,320 mls (3 733 km) at 482 mph (776 km/h) average at 37,700–44,600 ft (11 500–13 600 m).

Weights: Empty, 25,980 lb (11 795 kg); max. take-off (field), 60,400 lb (27 420 kg), (catapult), 58,600 lb (26 605 kg).

Armament: Five external (one fuselage and four wing) stations each of 3,600 lb (1 635 kg) capacity for up to 15,000 lb (6 804 kg) of stores.

Status: Current production version of the Intruder, the A-6E, first flew on February 27, 1970, and as of September 1975, 66 new A-6Es had been built and 104 modified from A-6A standard. Programme calls for last of 94 new-build A-6Es to be delivered in February 1976, and conversion of earlier Intruders to A-6E standard (total of 228) to extend through 1979.

Notes: All US Navy and US Marine Corps Intruders are being progressively updated to the latest A-6E standard with TRAM (Trails, Roads Interdiction Multi-sensor) systems, FLIR (Forward-Looking Infra-Red), provision for Rockwell AGM-53A Condor air-to-surface missiles and CAINS (Carrier Airborne Inertial Navigation System). The A-6E illustrated above is fitted with the Condor and that illustrated opposite is a new production A-6E with fuselage air brakes deleted and TRAM turret under nose.

GRUMMAN A-6E INTRUDER

Dimensions: Span, 53 ft 0 in (16,15 m); length, 54 ft 9 in (16,69 m); height, 16 ft 2 in (4,93 m); wing area, 528·9 sq ft (49,14 m²).

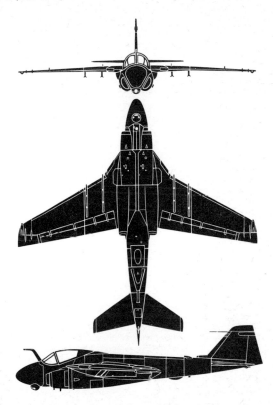

GRUMMAN E-2C HAWKEYE

Country of Origin: USA.

Type: Shipboard airborne early warning, surface surveillance and strike control aircraft.

Power Plant: Two 4,910 ehp Allison T56-A-422 turboprops.

Performance: Max. speed, 374 mph (602 km/h); normal cruise, 310 mph (499 km/h); mission endurance, 7 hrs, (at distance of 230 mls/370 km from base), 5 hrs; on-station loiter speed, 161 mph (259 km/h); ferry range, 1,605 mls (2 583 km); service ceiling, 30,800 ft (9 390 m).

Weights: Empty equipped, 37,678 lb (17 090 kg); max. take-off, 51,569 lb (23 391 kg).

Accommodation: Crew of five comprising flight crew of two and Airborne Tactical Data System team of three.

Status: First of two E-2C prototypes flown on January 20, 1971, with first production aircraft flying on September 23, 1972, total of 28 having been delivered by the beginning of 1976, with a further six funded for production during the year.

Notes: The E-2C is the current production version of the Hawkeye which first flew as an aerodynamic prototype on October 21, 1960. Fifty-nine examples of the E-2A (see 1968 edition) were delivered, all subsequently being updated to E-2B standards, the prototype of this version having flown on February 20, 1969. The 34th production E-2C, scheduled for delivery in November 1976, will be the first to receive the production ARPS (Advanced Radar Processing System) which will significantly improve the Hawkeye's capabilities and is to be retrofitted to all E-2Cs.

GRUMMAN E-2C HAWKEYE

Dimensions: Span, 80 ft 7 in (24,56 m); length, 57 ft 7 in (17,55 m); height, 18 ft 4 in (5,59 m); wing area, 700 sq ft (65,03 m²).

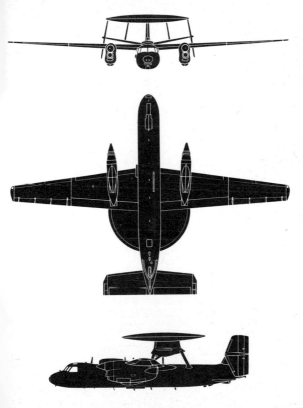

GRUMMAN F-14A TOMCAT

Country of Origin: USA.

Type: Two-seat shipboard multi-purpose fighter.

Power Plant: Two 20,900 lb (9 480 kg) reheat Pratt & Whitney TF30-P-412A turbofans.

Performance: Design max. speed (clean), 1,545 mph (2 486 km/h) at 40,000 ft (12 190 m) or Mach 2·34; max. speed (internal fuel and four AIM-7 missiles at 55,000 lb/24 948 kg), 910 mph (1 470 km/h) at sea level or Mach 1·2; tactical radius (internal fuel and four AIM-7 missiles plus allowance for 2 min combat at 10,000 ft/3 050 m), approx. 450 mls (725 km); time to 60,000 ft (18 290 m) at 55,000 lb (24 948 kg), 2·1 min.

Weights: Empty equipped, 40,070 lb (18 176 kg); normal take-off (internal fuel and four AIM-7 AAMs), 55,000 lb (24 948 kg); max. take-off (ground attack/interdiction), 68,567 lb (31 101 kg).

Armament: One 20-mm M-61A1 rotary cannon and (intercept mission) six AIM-7E/F Sparrow and four AIM-9G/H Sidewinder AAMs or six AIM-54A and two AIM-9G/H AAMs.

Status: First of 12 research and development aircraft flown December 21, 1970. Some 190 delivered by beginning of 1976 against anticipated procurement for US Navy of 378. Eighty ordered for Iran with deliveries commencing January 1976. Current production rate of 6–7 per month.

Notes: First of two F-14B prototypes powered by 28,096 lb (12 745 kg) reheat Pratt & Whitney F401-PW-400 turbofans flown on September 12, 1973. No production plans for this version exist. Plans to re-equip four US Marine Corps squadrons with the Tomcat were abandoned during the autumn of 1975.

GRUMMAN F-14A TOMCAT

Dimensions: Span (max.), 64 ft $1\frac{1}{2}$ in (19,55 m), (min.), 37 ft 7 in (11,45 m), (overswept on deck), 33 ft $3\frac{1}{2}$ in (10,15 m); length, 61 ft $11\frac{7}{8}$ in (18,90 m); height, 16 ft 0 in (4,88 m); wing area, 565 sq ft (52,5 m^2).

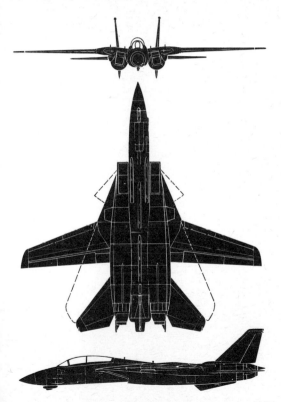

HAWKER SIDDELEY 125 SERIES 600

Country of Origin: United Kingdom.

Type: Light business executive transport.

Power Plant: Two 3,750 lb (1 700 kg) Rolls-Royce Viper 601 turbojets.

Performance: Max. cruise, 518 mph (834 km/h) at 27,000 ft (8 230 m); long-range cruise, 503 mph (810 km/h) at 40,000 ft (12 192 m); range (max. fuel and 1,600-lb/725-kg payload plus 45 min reserves), 1,876 mls (3 020 km), (with 2,359-lb/1 070-kg payload), 1,785 mls (2 872 km).

Weights: Empty equipped, 12,148 lb (5 510 kg); max. take-off, 25,000 lb (11 340 kg).

Accommodation: Normal flight crew of two and basic arrangement for eight passengers with alternative arrangements available for up to 14 passengers.

Status: Two Series 600 development aircraft flown on January 21, 1971, and November 25, 1971. Production deliveries began early 1973.

Notes: The Series 600 is the current production version of the basic HS.125, this being essentially a higher-powered, stretched version of the Series 400 which it replaced. An additional 2-ft (0,62-m) section was inserted in the fuselage ahead of the wing leading edge, allowing two more seats in the cabin; a nose radome of improved profile was adopted; the upper fuselage contours were revised, and taller vertical tail surfaces were introduced. Aircraft completed to US standards are designated Series 600A. Series 600 preceded by 101 Series 400 aircraft and 148 examples of earlier models plus two prototypes and 20 of a navigational training version (Dominie). A prototype Series 700 with Garrett TFE731 turbofans is expected to fly during 1976.

HAWKER SIDDELEY 125 SERIES 600

Dimensions: Span, 47 ft 0 in (14,32 m); length, 50 ft 5¾ in (15,37 m); height, 17 ft 3 in (5,26 m); wing area, 353 sq ft (32,8 m²).

HAWKER SIDDELEY 748 SERIES 2A

Country of Origin: United Kingdom.

Type: Short- to medium-range commercial transport.

Power Plant: Two 2,280 ehp Rolls-Royce Dart R.Da.7 Mk. 532-2L turboprops.

Performance: Max. speed at 40,000 lb (18 145 kg), 312 mph (502 km/h) at 16,000 ft (4 875 m); max. cruise, 287 mph (462 km/h) at 15,000 ft (4 570 m); econ. cruise, 267 mph (430 km/h) at 20,000 ft (6 095 m); range cruise, 259 mph (418 km/h) at 25,000 ft (7 620 m); range with max. fuel and reserves for 45 min hold and 230-mile (370-km) diversion, 1,862 mls (2 996 km), with max. payload and same reserves, 690 mls (1 110 km).

Weights: Basic operational, 25,361 lb (11 504 kg); max. take-off, 44,495 lb (20 182 kg).

Accommodation: Normal flight crew of two and standard cabin arrangement for 40 passengers on paired seats.

Status: First prototype flown June 24, 1960, and first production model (Series 1) on August 30, 1961. Series 1 superseded by Series 2 in 1962, this being in turn superseded by current Series 2A from mid-1967. Total of 309 ordered by beginning of 1976.

Notes: Assembled under licence in India by HAL for Indian Airlines (17) and Indian Air Force (four Series 1 and 58 Series 2), the last-mentioned figure including 10 ordered during 1975. The Series 2C flown on December 31, 1971, is similar to the Series 2A apart from the addition of a large freight door. Recent purchasers of the military version include the Belgian Air Force, which was taking delivery of three Series 2A freighters at the beginning of 1976.

HAWKER SIDDELEY 748 SERIES 2A

Dimensions: Span, 98 ft 6 in (30,02 m); length, 67 ft 0 in (20,42 m); height, 24 ft 10 in (7,57 m); wing area, 810·75 sq ft (75,35 m²).

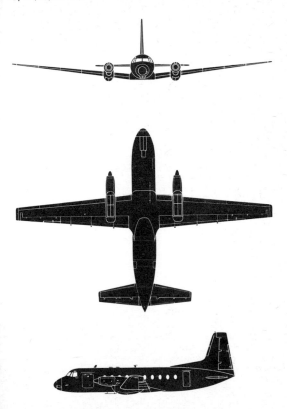

HAWKER SIDDELEY BUCCANEER
S. MK. 2B

Country of Origin: United Kingdom.
Type: Two-seat strike and reconnaissance aircraft.
Power Plant: Two 11,100 lb (5 035 kg) Rolls-Royce RB. 168-1A Spey Mk. 101 turbofans.
Performance: (Estimated) Max. speed, 645 mph (1 040 km/h) or Mach 0·85 at 250 ft (75 m), 620 mph (998 km/h) or Mach 0·92 at 30,000 ft (9 145 m); typical low-level cruise, 570 mph (917 km/h) or Mach 0·75 at 3,000 ft (915 m); tactical radius for hi-lo-lo-hi mission with standard fuel, 500—600 mls (805—965 km).
Weights: Max. take-off, 59,000 lb (26 762 kg).
Armament: Max. ordnance load of 16,000 lb (7 257 kg), including four 500-lb (227-kg), 540-lb (245-kg), or 1,000-lb (453,5-kg) bombs internally, and up to three 1,000-lb (453,5-kg) or six 500-lb (227-kg) bombs on each of four wing stations.
Status: First S. Mk. 2B for RAF flown January 8, 1970, with deliveries of 42 built to this standard continuing into 1976. Proportion of 84 S. Mk. 2s built for Royal Navy being modified for RAF use as S. Mk. 2As, and most of these ultimately to be converted to S. Mk. 2Bs.
Notes: The S. Mk. 2A embodies avionic, system and equipment modifications for RAF service. Wing and weapon-pylon changes to provide Martel missile capability characterise the S. Mk. 2B which introduces 425 Imp gal (1 932 l) fuel tank on rotating bomb door (seen on accompanying drawing) and undercarriage changes to accommodate new gross weight of 59,000 lb (26 762 kg). The Navy versions are S. Mk. 2C and S. Mk. 2D without and with Martel respectively.

HAWKER SIDDELEY BUCCANEER S. MK. 2B

Dimensions: Span, 44 ft 0 in (13,41 m); length, 63 ft 5 in (19,33 m); height, 16 ft 3 in (4,95 m); wing area, 514·7 sq ft (47,82 m²).

HAWKER SIDDELEY HARRIER G.R. MK. 3

Country of Origin: United Kingdom.
Type: Single-seat V/STOL strike and reconnaissance fighter.
Power Plant: One 21,500 lb (9 760 kg) Rolls-Royce Bristol Pegasus 103 vectored-thrust turbofan.
Performance: Max. speed, 720 mph (1 160 km/h) or Mach 0·95 at 1,000 ft (305 m), with typical external ordnance load, 640–660 mph (1 030–1 060 km) or Mach 0·85–0·87 at 1,000 ft (305 m); cruise, 560 mph (900 km/h) or Mach 0·8 at 20,000 ft (6 096 m); tactical radius for hi-lo-hi mission, 260 mls (418 km), with two 100 Imp gal (455 l) external tanks, 400 mls (644 km).
Weights: Empty, 12,400 lb (5 624 kg); max. take-off (VTO), 18,000 lb (8 165 kg); max. take-off (STO), 23,000+ lb (10 433+ kg); approx. max. take-off, 26,000 lb (11 793 kg).
Armament: Provision for two 30-mm Aden cannon with 130 rpg and up to 5,000 lb (2 268 kg) of ordnance.
Status: First of six pre-production aircraft flown August 31, 1966, with first of 77 G.R. Mk. 1s for RAF following December 28, 1967. Production of G.R. Mk. 1s and 13 T. Mk. 2s (see 1969 edition) for RAF completed. Production of 102 Mk. 50s (equivalent to G.R. Mk. 3) and eight Mk. 54 two-seaters (equivalent to T. Mk. 4) for US Marine Corps continuing into 1976, and six Mk. 50s and two Mk. 54s ordered (via the USA) by Spain. Follow-on order for 15 G.R. Mk. 3s placed March 1973.
Notes: RAF Harrier G.R. Mk. 1s and T. Mk. 2s converted to G.R. Mk. 1As and T. Mk. 2As by installation of 20,000 lb (9 100 kg) Pegasus 102. These are to be progressively modified as G.R. Mk. 3s and T. Mk. 4s by installation of Pegasus 103 similar to that installed in Mk. 50 (AV-8A) for USMC.

HAWKER SIDDELEY HARRIER G.R. MK. 3

Dimensions: Span, 25 ft 3 in (7,70 m); length, 45 ft 7$\frac{3}{4}$ in (13,91 m); height, 11 ft 3 in (3,43 m); wing area, 201·1 sq ft (18,68 m²).

HAWKER SIDDELEY HAWK T. MK. 1

Country of Origin: United Kingdom.

Type: Two-seat multi-purpose trainer and light tactical aircraft.

Power Plant: One 5,340 lb (2 422 kg) Rolls-Royce Turboméca RT.172-06-11 Adour 151 turbofan.

Performance: Max. speed, 617 mph (993 km/h) at sea level, 570 mph (917 km/h) at 30,000 ft (9 144 m); range cruise, 405 mph (652 km/h) at 30,000 ft (9 144 m); time to 40,000 ft (12 192 m), 10 min; service ceiling, 44,000 ft (13 410 m).

Weights: Empty, 7,450 lb (3 379 kg); normal take-off (trainer), 10,250 lb (4 649 kg), (weapons trainer), 12,000 lb (5 443 kg); max. take-off, 16,500 lb (7 484 kg).

Armament: (Weapon trainer) One strong point on fuselage centreline and two wing strong points and (ground attack) two additional wing strong points, all stressed for loads up to 1,000 lb (454 kg). Max. external load of 5,000 lb (2 268 kg).

Status: Single pre-production example flown on August 21, 1974, and first and second production examples flown on May 19 and April 22, 1975, respectively. Total of 175 on order for RAF with 10 being scheduled for delivery to that service during 1976 and production then running at 3–4 per month until completion of order in 1980.

Notes: The Hawk is to be used by the RAF in the basic and advanced flying training and weapons training roles, and both single- and two-seat ground attack versions are being offered for export. The projected single-seat version features more internal fuel, an automatic navigation system and various sensors to enhance weapon delivery.

HAWKER SIDDELEY HAWK T. MK. 1

Dimensions: Span, 30 ft 10 in (9,40 m); length (including probe), 39 ft 2½ in (11,96 m); height, 13 ft 5 in (4,10 m); wing area, 180 sq ft (16,70 m²).

HAWKER SIDDELEY NIMROD M.R. MK. 1

Country of Origin: United Kingdom.
Type: Long-range maritime patrol aircraft.
Power Plant: Four 12,160 lb (5 515 kg) Rolls-Royce RB. 168-20 Spey Mk. 250 turbofans.
Performance: Max. speed, 575 mph (926 km/h); max. transit speed, 547 mph (880 km/h); econ. transit speed, 490 mph (787 km/h); typical ferry range, 5,180–5,755 mls (8 340–9 265 km); typical endurance, 12 hrs.
Weights: Max. take-off, 177,500 lb (80 510 kg); max. overload (eight new-build Mk. 1s), 192,000 lb (87 090 kg).
Armament: Ventral weapons bay accommodating full range of ASW weapons (homing torpedoes, mines, depth charges, etc) plus two underwing pylons on each side for total of four Aérospatiale AS.12 ASMs (or AS.11 training rounds).
Accommodation: Normal operating crew of 12 with two pilots and flight engineer on flight deck and nine navigators and sensor operators in tactical compartment.
Status: First of two Nimrod prototypes employing modified Comet 4C airframes flown May 23, 1967. First of initial batch of 38 production Nimrod M.R. Mk. 1s flown on June 28, 1968. Completion of this batch in August 1972 followed by delivery of three Nimrod R. Mk. 1s for special electronics reconnaissance, and eight more M.R. Mk. 1s on order with deliveries continuing into 1976.
Notes: Entire fleet to undergo refit programme as Nimrod M.R. Mk. 2s with updated avionics and communications fit and service entry from 1978. Changes will include new EMI radar, a new sonics system, a navigation system of improved accuracy, increased computer capacity and improved display system techniques.

114

HAWKER SIDDELEY NIMROD M.R. MK. 1

Dimensions: Span, 114 ft 10 in (35,00 m); length, 126 ft 9 in (38,63 m); height, 29 ft 8½ in (9,01 m); wing area, 2,121 sq ft (197,05 m²).

HAWKER SIDDELEY TRIDENT 2E

Country of Origin: United Kingdom.
Type: Medium-haul commercial transport.
Power Plant: Three 11,930 lb (5 411 kg) Rolls-Royce RB.163-25 Mk. 512-5W/50 turbofans.
Performance: Max. cruise, 596 mph (959 km/h) at 30,000 ft (9 144 m); long-range cruise, 504 mph (891 km/h) at 35,000 ft (10 668 m); range with max. payload (29 600 lb/13 426 kg), 3,155 mls (5 077 km), with max. fuel at long-range cruise, 3,558 mls (5 726 km).
Weights: Operational empty, 73,200 lb (33 203 kg); max. take-off, 143,500 lb (65,090 kg).
Accommodation: Flight crew of three and alternative arrangements for 12 first-class and 79 or (British Airways) 97 tourist-class in six-abreast seating.
Status: Principal current production model of the Trident at the beginning of 1976 was the 2E which was being built against orders for 33 (plus two Super 3Bs) for the People's Republic of China. The first Trident 2E flew on July 27, 1967, 15 subsequently being delivered to British Airways (BEA) and two to Cyprus Airways.
Notes: The Trident 2E differs from the earlier Trident 1C and 1E (see 1966 edition) in having uprated engines, increased weights, Küchemann wingtips and increased span, fuel and weights. Twenty-four Trident 1Cs and 15 1Es were built. The Trident 3B (see 1973 edition) is a high-capacity short-haul development of the Trident 1E with a stretched fuselage and similar power plants and wing modifications to those of the 2E. Twenty-six Trident 3Bs were built for British Airways. The Super 3B offers accommodation for 152 passengers and carries additional fuel in the wing centre section.

116

HAWKER SIDDELEY TRIDENT 2E

Dimensions: Span, 98 ft 0 in (29,87 m); length, 114 ft 9 in (34,97 m); height, 27 ft 0 in (8,23 m); wing area, 1,462 sq ft (135,82 m²).

IAI 201 ARAVA

Country of Origin: Israel.

Type: Light STOL military transport.

Power Plant: Two 750 shp Pratt & Whitney (Canada) PT6A-34 turboprops.

Performance: Max. speed, 203 mph (326 km/h) at 10,000 ft (3 050 m); max. cruise, 198 mph (319 km/h) at 10,000 ft (3 050 m); econ. cruise, 193 mph (311 km/h); range (with max. fuel and 45 min reserves), 806 mls (1 297 km), (max. payload and 45 min reserves), 201 mls (323 km); initial climb, 1,270 ft/min (6,45 m/sec); service ceiling, 24,000 ft (7 315 m).

Weights: Basic operational, 8,816 lb (3 999 kg); max. take-off, 15,000 lb (6 803 kg).

Accommodation: Flight crew of one or two and up to 24 fully-equipped troops or 16 paratroops and two despatchers. Alternative interior arrangements include aeromedical version for 12 stretchers and two attendants.

Status: Prototype IAI 201 flown on March 7,1972 (first IAI 101 prototype having flown on November 27, 1969), and production running at two-three per month at beginning of 1976.

Notes: The IAI 201 is the military derivative of the IAI 101 Arava and has been ordered by Bolivia, Ecuador, El Salvador, Mexico and Nicaragua.

IAI 201 ARAVA

Dimensions: Span, 68 ft 6 in (20,88 m); length, 42 ft 6 in (12,95 m); height, 17 ft 1 in (5,21 m); wing area, 470·2 sq ft (43,68 m²).

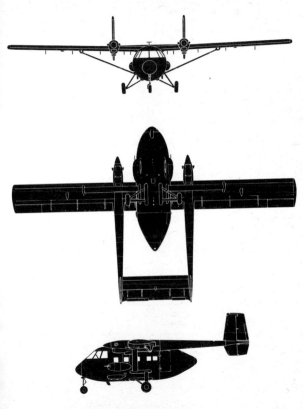

IAI KFIR

Country of Origin: Israel.

Type: Single-seat multi-role fighter.

Power Plant: One 11.870 lb (5 385 kg) dry and 17,900 lb (8 120 kg) IAI-built General Electric J79-GE-17 turbojet.

Performance: (Estimated) Max. speed, 850 mph (1 368 km/h) at low altitude or Mach 1·12, 1,450 mph (2 335 km/h) above 36,000 ft (10 970 m) or Mach 2·2; radius of action (lo-lo-lo), 375 mls (600 km), (hi-lo-hi), 810 mls (1 300 km), (M = 2·0 intercept with two 132 Imp gal/600 l external tanks), 230 mls (370 km); max. climb, 45,280 ft/min (230 m/sec).

Weights: (Estimated) Empty (interceptor), 15,873 (7 200 kg); loaded (interceptor), 23,590 lb (10 700 kg); max. take-off (ground attack), 31,980 lb (14 505 kg).

Armament: Two 30-mm IAI-manufactured DEFA cannon and (intercept) four Rafael Shafrir (Dragonfly) IR-guided missiles, or (ground attack) up to 8,820 lb (4 000 kg) of external stores, including Rockwell International Hobo guided bombs and Hughes Maverick ASMs.

Status: First prototype (Mirage conversion) flown in September 1971 as the Nesher (Eagle). Renamed Barak (Lightning) during development. Production initiated 1972-73 and assigned the appellation Kfir (Lion Cub) in 1975.

Notes: Based on the Dassault-Breguet Mirage 5 airframe, the J79-engined Kfir enjoys an appreciably improved thrust-to-weight ratio and is being produced in two versions differing primarily in the avionics installed and optimised respectively for the intercept/air superiority and ground attack roles respectively. Production was reportedly four per month late 1975 when it was announced that the Kfir would be available for export from mid-1977.

IAI KFIR

Dimensions: Span, 26 ft 11½ in (8,22 m); length, 51 ft 0¼ in (15,55 m); height, 13 ft 11½ in (4.25 m); wing area, 375·12 sq ft (34,85 m²).

IAI 1124 WESTWIND

Country of Origin: Israel.

Type: Light business executive transport.

Power Plant: Two 3,700 lb (1 680 kg) Garrett AiResearch TFE 731-3 turbofans.

Performance: Max. speed, 540 mph (869 km/h) at 19,400 ft (5 917 m) or Mach 0·735; range (seven passengers and 30 min reserves), 2,650 mls (4 264 km); max. fuel range (with 30 min reserves), 2,875 mls (4 626 km); initial climb, 4,000 ft/min (20,3 m/sec); service ceiling, 45,000 ft (13 725 m).

Weights: Operational empty, 12,700 lb (5 766 kg); max. take-off, 22,850 lb (10 374 kg).

Accommodation: Standard seating for two pilots on flight deck and seven passengers in main cabin (four individual seats and a three-place divan).

Status: Prototype flown on July 21, 1975, with customer deliveries scheduled for spring 1976. Production of initial batch of 36 commenced with production rate of three per month planned.

Notes: The Model 1124 Westwind differs from the Model 1123 primarily in having turbofans replacing the General Electric CJ-610-9 turbojets of the earlier model, a new wing leading edge, a strengthened undercarriage and a redesigned cockpit. The earlier Model 1123 Westwind was a developed version of the Jet Commander, all production and marketing rights in which were transferred to Israel Aircraft Industries. Production of a total of 36 examples of the Model 1123 was completed during the course of 1975.

IAI 1124 WESTWIND

Dimensions: Span, 44 ft 9½ in (13,65 m); length, 52 ft 3 in (15,94 m); height, 15 ft 9½ in (4,80 m); wing area, 308·3 sq ft (28,64 m²).

ILYUSHIN IL-38 (MAY)

Country of Origin: USSR.

Type: Long-range maritime patrol aircraft.

Power Plant: Four 4,250 ehp Ivchenko AI-20M turboprops.

Performance: (Estimated) Max. continuous cruise, 400 mph (645 km/h) at 15,000 ft (4 570 m); normal cruise, 370 mph (595 km/h) at 26,250 ft (8 000 m); patrol speed, 250 mph (400 km/h) at 2,000 ft (610 m); max. range, 4,500 mls (7 240 km); loiter endurance, 12 hrs at 2,000 ft (610 m).

Weights: (Estimated) Empty equipped, 80,000 lb (36 287 kg); max. take-off, 140,000 lb (63 500 kg).

Armament: Internal weapons bay for depth bombs, homing torpedoes, etc. Wing hardpoints for external ordnance loads.

Accommodation: Normal flight crew believed to consist of 12 members, of which half are housed by tactical compartment, operating sensors and co-ordinating data flow to surface vessels and other aircraft.

Status: The Il-38 reportedly flew in prototype form during 1967–68, entering service with the Soviet naval air arm early in 1970.

Notes: The Il-38 has been evolved from the Il-18 commercial transport in a similar fashion to the development of the Lockheed P-3 Orion from the Electra transport. Apart from some strengthening, the wings, tail assembly and undercarriage are similar to those of the Il-18. By comparison, the wing is positioned further forward on the fuselage for CG reasons. The Il-38 has been observed operating in the Mediterranean as well as over the seas surrounding the Soviet Union and an initial batch of three aircraft of this type is to be delivered to the Indian Navy during 1976.

124

ILYUSHIN IL-38 (MAY)

Dimensions: Span, 122 ft 9 in (37,40 m); length, 131 ft 0 in (39,92 m); height, 33 ft 4 in (10,17 m); wing area, 1,507 sq ft (140,0 m²).

ILYUSHIN IL-76 (CANDID)

Country of Origin: USSR.

Type: Heavy commercial and military freighter.

Power Plant: Four 26,455 lb (12 000 kg) Soloviev D-30KP turbofans.

Performance: Max. cruise, 528 mph (850 km/h) at 42,650 ft (13 000 m); range with max. payload (88,185 lb/40 000 kg), 3,107 mls (5 000 km).

Weights: Max. take-off, 346,122 lb (157 000 kg).

Accommodation: Normal flight crew of three—four with navigator below flight deck in glazed nose. Pressurised hold for containerised and other freight, wheeled and tracked vehicles, etc.

Status: First of four prototypes flown on March 25, 1971, with production deliveries to both Aeroflot and the Soviet Air Forces commencing in 1974.

Notes: The Il-76 is being manufactured in both commercial and military versions, the latter featuring tail warning radar and a tail gun position mounting two 23-mm NR-23 cannon. During the summer of 1975, an Il-76 established 25 new speed-with-load and load-to-altitude records, these including a 154,324-lb (70 000-kg) load over a distance of 621 mls (1 000 km) at an average speed of 532 mph (856 km/h), a similar load to an altitude of 38,959 ft (11 875 m), and a 88,185-lb (40 000-kg) load over a 3,107-mile (5 000-km) closed circuit at an average speed of 507 mph (816 km/h).

ILYUSHIN IL-76 (CANDID)

Dimensions: Span, 165 ft 8⅓ in (50,50 m); length, 152 ft 10¼ in (46,59 m); height, 48 ft 5⅛ in (14,76 m); wing area, 3,229·2 sq ft (300,00 m²).

ILYUSHIN IL-86

Country of Origin: USSR.

Type: Medium-haul commercial transport.

Power Plant: Four 28,660 lb (13 000 kg) Soloviev (or Lotarev) turbofans.

Performance: (Estimated) Normal cruise, 572–590 mph (920–950 km/h) at 30,000–33,000 ft (9 000–10 000 m); range with max. payload (88,185 lb/40 000 kg), 1,460 mls (2 350 km), with max. fuel, 2,858 mls (4 600 km).

Weights: Max. take-off, 414,470 lb (188 000 kg).

Accommodation: Flight crew of three–four and up to 350 passengers in basic nine-abreast seating with two aisles (divided between three cabins accommodating 111, 141 and 98 passengers respectively). One proposed mixed-class layout provides for 28 passengers six-abreast in forward cabin and 206 passengers eight-abreast in centre and aft cabins.

Status: Prototype scheduled to fly during the course of 1976, with Aeroflot service entry expected towards the end of the present decade.

Notes: Evolved under the supervision of General Designer G. V. Novozhilov, the IL-86 is intended for both domestic and international high-density routes. The prototype is expected to be powered by four Soloviev D-30KP turbofans of 26,455 lb (12 000 kg) each, but an uprated turbofan of Soloviev design or a competitive turbofan from the Lotarev bureau is expected to power the initial production version. The IL-86 will be operated by Aeroflot over stage lengths ranging from 500 to 2,360 miles (800 to 3 800 km).

ILYUSHIN IL-86

Dimensions: Span, 158 ft 6 in (48,33 m); length, 191 ft 11 in (58,50 m); height, 51 ft 6 in (15,70 m); wing area, 3,444 sq ft (320,0 m²).

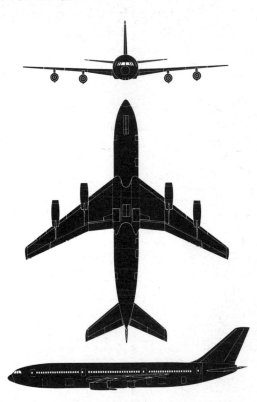

JUROM ORAO

Countries of Origin: Jugoslavia and Romania.
Type: Single-seat tactical fighter and two-seat operational trainer.
Power Plant: Two 4,000 lb (1 814 kg) Rolls-Royce Viper 623 turbojets.
Performance: (Estimated) Max. speed, 700 mph (1 126 km/h) or Mach 0·92 at sea level, 627 mph (1 010 km/h) or Mach 0·95 at 40,000 ft (12 190 m); radius of action with 4,410-lb (2 000-kg) warload (lo-lo-lo), 155 mls (250 km), (hi-lo-hi), 280 mls (450 km); initial climb, 17,700 ft/min (90 m/sec); service ceiling, 44,290 ft (13 500 m).
Weights: (Estimated) Empty equipped, 9,700 lb (4 400 kg); max. take-off, 19,840 lb (9 000 kg).
Armament: Two 30-mm cannon and up to 4,410 lb (2 000 kg) of ordnance on five external stations.
Status: First of two prototypes flown in August 1974, with pre-production series under construction at beginning of 1976. Anticipated production of up to 200 aircraft for each of the Jugoslav and Romanian air arms with deliveries commencing 1977–78.
Notes: The Orao (Eagle) is being developed jointly by the Jugoslav and Romanian (JuRom) aircraft industries, the Jugoslavian SOKO organisation being team leader. Several versions of the Orao are currently projected, including the single-seat tactical fighter (illustrated), both single- and two-seat tactical reconnaissance models, and a two-seat conversion trainer retaining full operational capability. Components for the Orao are being manufactured by both the Jugoslav and Romanian industries as single-source suppliers, but it is anticipated that only one assembly line will be established (in Jugoslavia).

130

JUROM ORAO

Dimensions: (Estimated) Span, 24 ft 7 in (7,50 m); length, 42 ft 8 in (13,00 m); height, 12 ft 1½ in (3,70 m); wing area, 193·75 sq ft (18,00 m²).

KAWASAKI C-1A

Country of Origin: Japan.

Type: Medium-range military transport.

Power Plant: Two 14,500 lb (6 575 kg) Pratt & Whitney JT8D-9 turbofans.

Performance: Max. speed (at 78,264 lb/35 500 kg), 507 mph (816 km/h) at 25,000 ft (7 620 m); max. cruise, 437 mph (703 km/h) at 35,000 ft (10 670 m); econ. cruise, 386 mph (621 km/h) at 35,000 ft (10 670 m); range with normal payload (17,637 lb/8 000 kg), 807 mls (1 300 km), with max. fuel and 5,730-lb (2 600-kg) payload, 2,073 mls (3 336 km); initial climb (at 99,208 lb/45 000 kg), 3,500 ft/min (17,78 m/sec); service ceiling, 40,000 ft (12 190 m).

Weights: Empty, 51,036 lb (23 150 kg); empty equipped, 53,131 lb (24 100 kg); normal loaded, 85,980 lb (39 000 kg); max. take-off, 99,208 lb (45 000 kg).

Accommodation: Basic crew of five. Typical loads include 60 troops, 45 paratroops, 36 casualty stretchers, three jeeps, a 2·5-ton truck and a 2-ton trailer, or a 106-mm self-propelled gun.

Status: First of two prototypes flown November 12, 1970, and first of two pre-production aircraft delivered December 1973, with first production example following one year later. Twenty-four production examples so far funded with last to be delivered February 1978.

Notes: Minelaying version currently projected.

KAWASAKI C-1A

Dimensions: Span, 100 ft 3¾ in (30,60 m); length, 95 ft 1¼ in (29,00 m); height, 32 ft 9¾ in (10,00 m); wing area, 1,297 sq ft (120,50 m²).

LET L 410 TURBOLET

Country of Origin: Czechoslovakia.

Type: Light utility transport, feederliner and (L 410AF) photographic survey aircraft.

Power Plant: Two 715 ehp Pratt & Whitney (Canada) PT6A-27 turboprops.

Performance: Max. cruise, 235 mph (380 km/h) at 9,840 ft (3 000 m); econ. cruise, 205 mph (330 km/h) at 9,840 ft (3 000 m); range with max. fuel and 45 min reserves, 705 mls (1 140 km), with max. payload and same reserves, 115 mls (185 km); initial climb, 1,595 ft/min (8,1 m/sec); service ceiling, 25,490 ft (7 770 m).

Weights: Basic empty (freight version), 6,876 lb (3 100 kg); max. take-off, 11,905 lb (5 400 kg).

Accommodation: Flight crew of two and alternative arrangements for 12, 15, 19 or 20 passengers in rows of three with two seats to starboard and one to port. L 410AF photographic version has stations for camera operators in nose and main cabin.

Status: First of four prototypes flown April 16, 1969. Pre-production series of six aircraft built during 1971 of which two entered service with Slov-Air in September of that year. First production deliveries (to Slov-Air) commenced in 1972, and photographic versions developed in 1973 with first deliveries (to Hungary) in 1974.

Notes: Development of variant with the indigenous M-601-B turboprop of 740 ehp continuing at beginning of 1976. The accompanying general arrangement silhouette depicts the photographic L410AF which features a fixed nosewheel.

LET L 410 TURBOLET

Dimensions: Span, 57 ft 3 in (17,50 m); length, 44 ft 7½ in (13,61 m); height, 18 ft 4 in (5,65 m); wing area, 349·83 sq ft (32,5 m²).

LOCKHEED L-1011-200 TRISTAR

Country of Origin: USA.

Type: Medium- to long-haul commercial transport.

Power Plant: Three 48,000 lb (21 772 kg) Rolls-Royce RB.211-524 turbofans.

Performance: (At 360,000 lb/163 290 kg) Max. cruise, 608 mph (978 km/h) at 31,000 ft (9 450 m); econ. cruise, 567 mph (913 km/h) at 31,000 ft (9 450 m); long-range cruise, 557 mph (896 km/h); range (at 466,000 lb/211 375 kg) with 74,200-lb (33 657-kg) payload, 4,887 mls (7 865 km), with max. fuel and 42,827-lb (19 426-kg) payload, 6,208 mls (9 992 km).

Weights: Operational empty, 245,800 lb (111 493 kg); max. take-off, 466,000 lb (211 375 kg).

Accommodation: Basic flight crew of three—four. Typical passenger configuration provides 256 seats in a ratio of 20% first class and 80% coach class. All-economy configurations provide for up to 400 passengers.

Status: L-1011-1 first flown November 16, 1970, with first deliveries (to Eastern) following in April 1972. Deliveries of the longer-range L-1011-100 initiated (to Cathay Pacific) August 1975, with the more powerful L-1011-200 scheduled to enter service (with Saudia) during 1976.

Notes: Externally identical and complementary to the basic L-1011-1, the L-1011-100 is available with either 42,000 lb (19 050 kg) RB.211-22B or 43,500 lb (19 730 kg) RB.211-22F engines, while the L-1011-200 described above features additional centre-section fuel tankage and RB.211-524 engines. The aircraft illustrated above was delivered to Saudia as an L-1011-100 but will be retrofitted with -524 engines during 1976 as an L-1011-200. The long-range L-1011-250 announced in 1975 will differ from the -200 in having a further increase in centre-section tankage and a take-off weight of 484,000 lb (219 540 kg).

LOCKHEED L-1011-200 TRISTAR

Dimensions: Span, 155 ft 4 in (47,34 m); length, 178 ft 8 in (54,35 m); height, 55 ft 4 in (16,87 m); wing area, 3,456 sq ft (320,0 m²).

LOCKHEED C-130H HERCULES

Country of Origin: USA.

Type: Medium- to long-range military transport.

Power Plant: Four 4,050 eshp Allison T56-A-7A turbo-props.

Performance: Max. speed, 384 mph (618 km/h); max. cruise, 368 mph (592 km/h); econ. cruise, 340 mph (547 km/h); range (with max. payload and 5% plus 30 min reserves), 2,450 mls (3 943 km); max. range, 4,770 mls (7 675 km); initial climb, 1,900 ft/min (9,65 m/sec).

Weights: Empty equipped, 72,892 lb (33 063 kg); max. normal take-off, 155,000 lb (70 310 kg); max. overload, 175,000 lb (79 380 kg).

Accommodation: Flight crew of four and max. of 92 fully-equipped troops, 64 paratroops, or 74 casualty stretchers and two medical attendants. As a cargo carrier up to six pre-loaded freight pallets may be carried.

Status: The C-130H is the principal current production version of the Hercules which, in progressively developed forms, has been in continuous production since 1952, and at the beginning of 1976, when some 1,350 Hercules had been ordered, production rate was six per month.

Notes: The C-130H, which was in process of delivery to the USAF, Greece, Israel, Malaysia, Saudi Arabia and Spain at the beginning of 1976, is basically a C-130E with more powerful engines, and the Hercules C Mk. 1 (C-130K) serving with the RAF differs in having some UK-supplied instruments, avionics and other items.

LOCKHEED C-130H HERCULES

Dimensions: Span, 132 ft 7 in (40,41 m); length, 97 ft 9 in (29,78 m); height, 38 ft 3 in (11,66 m); wing area, 1,745 sq ft (162,12 m²).

LOCKHEED P-3C ORION

Country of Origin: USA.

Type: Long-range maritime patrol aircraft.

Power Plant: Four 4,910 eshp Allison T56-A-14W turbo-props.

Performance: Max. speed at 105,000 lb (47 625 kg), 473 mph (761 km/h) at 15,000 ft (4 570 m); normal cruise, 397 mph (639 km/h) at 25,000 ft (7 620 ml); patrol speed, 230 mph (370 km/h) at 1,500 ft (457 m); loiter endurance (all engines) at 1,500 ft (457 m) 12·3 hours, (two engines), 17 hrs; max. mission radius, 2,530 mls (4 075 km), with 3 hrs on station at 1,500 ft (457 m), 1,933 mls (3 110 km); initial climb, 2,880 ft/min (14,6 m/sec).

Weights: Empty, 61,491 lb (27 890 kg); normal max. take-off, 133,500 lb (60 558 kg); max. overload, 142,000 lb (64 410 kg).

Accommodation: Normal flight crew of 10 of which five housed in tactical compartment. Up to 50 combat troops and 4,000 lb (1 814 kg) of equipment for trooping role.

Armament: Weapons bay can house two Mk 101 depth bombs and four Mk 43, 44 or 46 torpedoes, or eight Mk 54 bombs. External ordnance load of up to 13,713 lb (6 220 kg).

Status: YP-3C prototype flown October 8, 1968, P-3C deliveries commencing to US Navy mid-1969 with 130 delivered by 1976, and a further 12 aircraft per year to be ordered until at least 1985.

Notes: The P-3C differs from the P-3A (157 built) and -3B (145 built) primarily in having more advanced sensor equipment. Twelve P-3As have been modified as EP-3Es for the electronic reconnaissance role, others have been adapted for the weather reconnaissance role as WP-3As, and a specially-equipped version, the RP-3D, is being used to map the earth's magnetic field. Six Orions have been delivered to Iran as P-3Fs (illustrated above).

LOCKHEED P-3C ORION

Dimensions: Span, 99 ft 8 in (30,37 m); length, 116 ft 10 in (35,61 m); height, 33 ft 8½ in (10,29 m); wing area, 1,300 sq ft (120,77 m²).

LOCKHEED S-3A VIKING

Country of Origin: USA.

Type: Four-seat shipboard anti-submarine aircraft.

Power Plant: Two 9,280 lb (4 210 kg) General Electric TF34-GE-2 turbofans.

Performance: Max. speed, 506 mph (815 km/h) at sea level; max. cruise, 403 mph (649 km/h); typical loiter speed, 184 mph (257 km/h); max. ferry range, 3,500 mls (5 630 km) plus; initial climb, 3,937 ft/min (20 m/sec); service ceiling, 35,000 ft (10 670 m); sea level endurance, 7·5 hrs at 186 mph (300 km/h).

Weights: Empty equipped, 26,554 lb (12 044 kg); normal max. take-off, 43,491 lb (19 727 kg).

Accommodation: Pilot and co-pilot side by side on flight deck, with tactical co-ordinator and sensor operator in aft cabin. All four crew members provided with zero-zero ejection seats.

Armament: Various combinations of torpedoes, depth charges, bombs and ASMs in internal weapons bay and on underwing pylons.

Status: First of eight development and evaluation aircraft commenced its test programme on January 21, 1972, and remaining seven had flown by early 1973. Deliveries against follow-on orders for 138 scheduled for delivery at rate of four per month through 1976. Current US Navy planning calls for acquisition of 179 production aircraft by December 1977.

Notes: Intended as a successor to the Grumman S-2 Tracker in US Navy service, Lockheed's shipboard turbofan-powered ASW aircraft was selected for development mid-1969, and entered fleet service during the course of 1974.

LOCKHEED S-3A VIKING

Dimensions: Span, 68 ft 8 in (20,93 m); length, 53 ft 4 in (16,26 m); height, 22 ft 9 in (6,93 m); wing area, 598 sq ft (55,56 m²).

LTV AEROSPACE A-7E CORSAIR II

Country of Origin: USA.

Type: Single-seat shipboard tactical fighter.

Power Plant: One 15,000 lb (6 804 kg) Allison TF41-A-2 (Rolls-Royce RB. 168-62 Spey) turbofan.

Performance: Max. speed without external stores, 699 mph (1 125 km/h) or Mach 0·92 at sea level, with 12 250-lb (113,4-kg) bombs, 633 mph (1 020 km/h) or Mach 0·87 at sea level; tactical radius with 12 250-lb (113,4-kg) bombs for hi-lo-hi mission at average cruise of 532 mph (856 km/h) with 1 hr on station, 512 mls (825 km); ferry range on internal fuel, 2,775 mls (4 465 km).

Weights: Empty equipped, 17,569 lb (7 969 kg); max. take-off, 42,000+ lb (19 050+ kg).

Armament: One 20-mm M-61A-1 rotary cannon with 1,000 rounds and (for short-range interdiction) maximum ordnance load of 20,000 lb (9 072 kg).

Status: A-7E first flown November 25, 1968, with production deliveries to US Navy following mid-1969. First 67 delivered with Pratt & Whitney TF30-P-8 (subsequently redesignated A-7Cs). Planned procurement totals 706 aircraft.

Notes: A-7E is the shipboard equivalent of the USAF's A-7D (see 1970 edition). Preceded into service by A-7A (199 built) and A-7B (196 built) with 11,350 lb (5 150 kg) TF30-P-6 and 12,200 lb (5 534 kg) TF30-P-8 respectively. Eighty-one early Corsairs (40 A-7Bs and 41 A-7Cs) are being converted as tandem two-seat TA-7Cs for the training role. Delivery of 60 A-7Hs (equivalent to A-7D) to Greece commenced 1975.

LTV AEROSPACE A-7E CORSAIR II

Dimensions: Span, 38 ft 8¾ in (11,80 m); length, 46 ft 1½ in (14,06 m); height, 16 ft 0¾ in (4,90 m); wing area, 375 sq ft (34,83 m²).

McDONNELL DOUGLAS DC-9 SERIES 50

Country of Origin: USA.

Type: Short-to-medium-haul commercial transport.

Power Plant: Two 16,000 lb (7 257 kg) Pratt & Whitney JT8D-17 turbofans.

Performance: Max. cruise, 564 mph (907 km/h) at 27,000 ft (8 230 m); econ. cruise, 535 mph (861 km/h) at 33,000 ft (10 060 m); long-range cruise, 509 mph (819 km/h) at 35,000 ft (10 668 m); range with max. payload (33,000 lb/ 14 950 kg), 1,468 mls (2 362 km), with max. fuel (and 21,400-lb/9 700-kg payload), 2,787 mls (4 485 km).

Weights: Operational empty, 65,000 lb (29 484 kg); max. take-off, 120,000 lb (54 430 kg).

Accommodation: Flight crew of two/three and maximum high-density arrangement for 139 passengers in five-abreast seating.

Status: The first DC-9 Series 50 flew on December 17, 1974, with first delivery (against initial order for 10 from Swissair) following during July 1975. Thirty-eight firm orders for the Series 50 had been received by the beginning of 1976, when total orders for all versions of the DC-9 amounted to 840 aircraft.

Notes: The latest of five basic DC-9 models, the Series 50 represents a further "stretch" of the basic DC-9 airframe, the fuselage being 6·4 ft (1,95 m) longer than the previously largest DC-9, the Series 40. The DC-9 was first flown on February 25, 1965, and the 700th aircraft of this type was delivered in July 1973. Production versions include the initial Series 10, the Series 20 (see 1969 edition) retaining the short fuselage of the Series 10 with the longer-span wing of the Series 30 (see 1973 edition) and the Series 40 (see 1972 edition). The Series 60 is projected with a further fuselage "stretch" and refanned engines.

146

McDONNELL DOUGLAS DC-9 SERIES 50

Dimensions: Span, 93 ft 5 in (28,47 m); length, 132 ft 0 in (40,23 m); height, 27 ft 6 in (8,38 m); wing area, 1,000·7 sq ft (92,97 m²).

McDONNELL DOUGLAS DC-10 SERIES 30

Country of Origin: USA.

Type: Medium-range commercial transport.

Power Plant: Three 51,000 lb (23 134 kg) General Electric CF6-50C turbofans.

Performance: Max. cruise (at 520,000 lb/235 868 kg), 570 mph (917 km/h) at 31,000 ft (9 450 m); long-range cruise, 554 mph (891 km/h) at 31,000 ft (9 450 m); max. fuel range (with 230 mls/370 km reserves), 6,909 mls (11 118 km); max. payload range, 4,272 mls (6 875 km); max. climb rate, 2,320 ft/min (11,78 m/sec); service ceiling (at 540,000 lb/244 940 kg), 32,700 ft (9 965 m).

Weights: Basic operating, 263,087 lb (119 334 kg); max. take-off, 555,000 lb (251 745 kg).

Accommodation: Flight crew of three plus provision on flight deck for two supernumerary crew. Typical mixed-class accommodation for 225–270 passengers. Max. authorised passenger accommodation, 380 (plus crew of 11).

Status: First DC-10 (Series 10) flown August 29, 1970, with first Series 30 (46th DC-10 built) flying June 21, 1972, being preceded on February 28, 1972, by first Series 40. Orders totalled 235 by December 1975, when some 20 remained to be delivered.

Notes: The DC-10 Series 30 and 40 have identical fuselages to the DC-10 Series 10 (see 1972 edition), but whereas the last-mentioned version is a domestic model, the Series 30 and 40 are intercontinental models, and differ in power plant, weight and wing details, and in the use of three main undercarriage units, the third (a twin-wheel unit) being mounted on the fuselage centreline. The Series 40 (illustrated above) has 49,400 lb (22 407 kg) Pratt & Whitney JT9D-20 turbofans but is otherwise similar to the Series 30.

McDONNELL DOUGLAS DC-10 SERIES 30

Dimensions: Span, 165 ft 4 in (50,42 m); length, 181 ft 4¾ in (55,29 m); height, 58 ft 0 in (17,68 m); wing area, 3,921·4 sq ft (364,3 m²).

McDONNELL DOUGLAS F-15 EAGLE

Country of Origin: USA.

Type: Single-seat air superiority fighter (F-15A) and two-seat operational trainer (TF-15A).

Power Plant: Two (approx.) 25,000 lb (11 340 kg) reheat Pratt & Whitney F100-PW-100 turbofans.

Performance: Max. speed, 915 mph (1 472 km/h) at sea level or Mach 1·2, 1,650 mph (2 655 km/h) at 36,090 ft (11 000 m) or Mach 2·5; tactical radius (combat air patrol), up to 1,120 mls (1 800 km); ferry range, 2,980 mls (4 800 km), (with Fast Pack auxiliary tanks), 3,450 mls (5 560 km).

Weights: Empty equipped, 26,147 lb (11 860 kg); loaded (clean), 38,250 lb (17 350 kg); max. take-off (intercept mission), 40,000 lb (18 145 kg); max. take-off, 54,123 lb (24 550 kg).

Armament: One 20-mm M-61A-1 rotary cannon with 950 rounds and (intercept mission) four AIM-9L Sidewinder and four AIM-7F Sparrow AAMs. Five stores stations (four wing and one fuselage) can lift up to 15,000 lb (6 804 kg) of ordnance.

Status: Twenty test and development aircraft ordered (18 F-15As and two TF-15As) with first F-15A flying on July 27, 1972, and first TF-15A on July 7, 1973. Current planning calls for acquisition of 729 Eagles by USAF, every seventh aircraft being a TF-15A. Delivery of 25 F-15As to Israel expected to commence January 1977.

150

McDONNELL DOUGLAS F-15 EAGLE

Dimensions: Span, 42 ft 9¾ in (13,05 m); length, 63 ft 9 in (19,43 m); height, 18 ft 5½ in (5,63 m); wing area, 608 sq ft (56,50 m²).

McDONNELL DOUGLAS F-4 PHANTOM

Country of Origin: USA.

Type: Two-seat interceptor and tactical strike fighter.

Power Plant: Two 11,870 lb (5 385 kg) dry and 17,900 lb (8 120 kg) reheat General Electric J79-GE-17 or (F-4F) MTU-built J79-MTU-17A turbojets.

Performance: (F-4E) Max. speed without external stores, 910 mph (1 464 km/h) or Mach 1·2 at 1,000 ft (305 m), 1,500 mph (2 414 km/h) or Mach 2·27 at 40,000 ft (12 190 m); tactical radius (with four Sparrow III and four Sidewinder AAMs), 140 mls (225 km), (plus one 500 Imp gal/2 273 l auxiliary tank), 196 mls (315 km), (hi-lo-hi mission profile with four 1,000-lb/453,6-kg bombs, four AAMs, and one 500 Imp gal/2 273 l and two 308 Imp gal/1 400 l tanks), 656 mls (1 056 km); max. ferry range, 2,300 mls (3 700 km) at 575 mph (925 km/h).

Weights: (F-4E) Empty equipped, 30,425 lb (13 801 kg); loaded (with four Sparrow IIIs), 51,810 lb (21 500 kg), (plus four Sidewinders and max. external fuel, 58,000 lb (26 308 kg); max. overload, 60,630 lb (27 502 kg).

Armament: One 20-mm M-61A1 rotary cannon and (intercept) four or six AIM-7E plus four AIM-9D AAMs, or (attack) up to 16,000 lb (7 257 kg) of external stores.

Status: First F-4E flown June 1967, and production continuing at beginning of 1974. First F-4F (for Federal Germany) completed May 1973 with deliveries through 1974. Phantom deliveries exceeded 4,700 by 1976.

Notes: Current production models of the Phantom in addition to the F-4E (see 1973 edition) are the RF-4E (see 1972 edition), the F-4EJ for Japan and the F-4F for Federal Germany. The last-mentioned version (illustrated on opposite page), optimised for the intercept role, entered service with the Luftwaffe from January 1, 1974, and features leading-edge slats and various weight-saving features.

McDONNELL DOUGLAS F-4 PHANTOM

Dimensions: Span, 38 ft 4¾ in (11,70 m); length, 62 ft 10½ in (19,20 m); height, 16 ft 3⅓ in (4,96 m); wing area, 530 sq ft (49,2 m²).

McDONNELL DOUGLAS A-4N SKYHAWK II

Country of Origin: USA.

Type: Single-seat light attack bomber.

Power Plant: One 11,200 lb (5 080 kg) Pratt & Whitney J52-P-408A turbojet.

Performance: Max. speed without external stores, 685 mph (1 102 km/h) or Mach 0·9 at sea level, 640 mph (1 030 km/h) at 25,000 ft (7 620 m), in high drag configuration, 625 mph (1 080 km/h) or Mach 0·82 at sea level, 605 mph (973 km/h) or Mach 0·84 at 30,000 ft (9 145 m); combat radius on internal fuel for hi-lo-lo-hi mission profile with 4,000 lb (1 814 kg) of external stores, 340 mls (547 km); initial climb, 15,850 ft/min (80,5 m/sec), at 23,000 lb (10 433 kg), 8,440 ft/min (42,7 m/sec).

Weights: Empty, 10,600 lb (4 808 kg); max. take-off, 24,500 lb (11 113 kg).

Armament: Two 30-mm DEFA cannon and external weapons loads up to 8,200 lb (3 720 kg) on wing and fuselage hardpoints.

Status: First A-4N flown June 12, 1972, with first production deliveries (to Israel) initiated November 1972. Production of similar A-4M (or A-4Y) to continue into 1977.

Notes: The A-4N employs essentially the same power plant and airframe as the A-4M (illustrated above), both models being referred to as the Skyhawk II. The A-4N embodies some of the features originally developed for the Israeli A-4H (e.g., twin 30-mm cannon) but has a new nav/attack system (similar to A-7D and -7E) and a revised cockpit layout. Thirty-six A-4M Skyhawks were ordered by Kuwait late 1974. All USMC A-4Ms are to be updated as A-4Ys with redesigned cockpit and revised systems.

McDONNELL DOUGLAS A-4N SKYHAWK II

Dimensions: Span, 27 ft 6 in (8,38 m); length, 40 ft 3¼ in (12,27 m); height, 15 ft 0 in (4,57 m); wing area, 260 sq ft (24,16 m²).

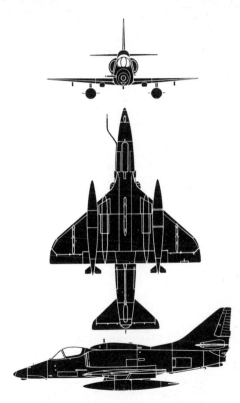

McDONNELL DOUGLAS YC-15

Country of Origin: USA.

Type: Medium STOL tactical transport.

Power Plant: Four 16,000 lb (7 258 kg) Pratt & Whitney JT8D-17 turbofans.

Performance: (Estimated) Max. speed, 535 mph (861 km/h); operational radius utilising STOL techniques with 27,000-lb (12 247-kg) payload or conventional techniques with 62,000-lb (28 122-kg) payload, 460 mls (740 km); ferry range, 2,992 mls (4 814 km).

Weights: Max. take-off, 216,680 lb (98 286 kg).

Accommodation: Flight crew of three. Hold can accommodate all US Army vehicles up to and including the 62,000-lb (28 123-kg) extended-barrel self-propelled 8-in (20,3-cm) howitzer. Approximately 150 fully-equipped troops may be carried or mix of troops and freight (eg, six freight pallets and 40 troops).

Status: First YC-15 flown August 26, 1975, with second following on December 5, 1975. The YC-15 will compete in a prototype fly-off contest with the Boeing YC-14 (see pages 50–51) during 1976–77, with production decision expected 1977–78.

Notes: McDonnell Douglas's contender for the USAF's advanced military STOL transport (AMST) requirement, the YC-15 derives short take-off and landing characteristics from a variety of high-lift devices, including double-slotted flaps over some 75% of the total wing span and operating directly in the exhaust stream from the widely-spaced turbofans. The YC-15 can operate into and out of 2,000-ft (610-m) runways.

McDONNELL DOUGLAS YC-15

Dimensions: Span, 110 ft 4 in (33,64 m); length, 124 ft 3 in (37,90 m); height, 43 ft 4 in (13,20 m); wing area, 1,740 sq ft (161,65 m²).

MIKOYAN MIG-21SMT (FISHBED-K)

Country of Origin: USSR.

Type: Single-seat multi-purpose fighter.

Power Plant: One 11,244 lb (5 100 kg) dry and 14,550 lb (6 600 kg) reheat Tumansky R-13 turbojet.

Performance: Max. speed, 808 mph (1 300 km/h) at 1,000 ft (305 m) or Mach 1·06, 1,386 mph (2 230 km/h) above 36,090 ft (11 000 m) or Mach 2·1; approx. range on internal fuel, 750 mls (1 207 km); endurance (with one centreline drop tank), 3·5 hrs; service ceiling, 59,055 ft (18 000 m).

Weights: Approx. normal take-off (with four K-13 AAMs), 18,500 lb (8 392 kg); approx. max. take-off, 21,000 lb (9 525 kg).

Armament: One twin-barrel 23-mm GSh-23 cannon with 200 rounds and up to four AAMs (Atoll and Advanced Atoll) on wing pylons for intercept role. Various external stores for ground attack, including UV-16-57 or UV-32-57 pods each containing 16 and 32 55-mm S-5 rockets respectively, 240-mm S-24 rockets or 550-lb (250-kg) bombs.

Status: The MiG-21SMT is a progressive development of the MiG-21MF (see 1974 edition) and began to enter service with the Soviet Air Forces in 1973.

Notes: Referred to as the "third generation" MiG-21, the MiG-21SMT differs from the MiG-21MF primarily in having revised upper fuselage contours resulting from the introduction of a "saddle" fuel tank to improve the previously inadequate range and endurance on internal fuel, leaving the wing pylons free for ordnance. The MiG-21SMT also reportedly features upgraded avionics.

MIKOYAN MIG-21SMT (FISHBED-K)

Dimensions: Span, 23 ft $5\frac{1}{2}$ in (7,15 m); length (including probe), 51 ft $8\frac{1}{2}$ in (15,76 m), (without probe), 44 ft 2 in (13,46 m); wing area, 247·57 sq ft (23,0 m²).

MIKOYAN MIG-23 (FLOGGER)

Country of Origin: USSR.

Type: Single-seat multi-role fighter and two-seat operational trainer.

Power Plant: One (estimated) 14,330 lb (6 500 kg) dry and 20,500 lb (9 300 kg) reheat Tumansky turbofan.

Performance: (Estimated) Max. speed, 865 mph at 1,000 ft (305 m) or Mach 1·2, 1,520 mph (2 446 km/h) above 39,370 ft (12 000 m) or Mach 2·3; tactical radius (hi-lo-hi with centre-line drop tank), 620 mls (1 000 km), (lo-lo-lo), 220 mls (350 km); time to 36,090 ft (11 000 m), 8·0 min; combat cruise at sea level, 645 mph (1 040 km/h) or Mach 0·85; max. range, 1,550 mls (2 500 km).

Weights: (Estimated) Normal loaded, 34,600 lb (15 700 kg); max. take-off, 39,130 lb (17 750 kg).

Armament: (Flogger-B) One 23-mm twin-barrel GSh-23 cannon plus two IR-homing and two radar-homing Atoll AAMs, or (Flogger-D) one 23-mm six-barrel rotary cannon and up to 6,600 lb (3 000 kg) of ordnance on five external stations.

Status: The MiG-23 is believed to have first entered service during 1971, and in addition to the Soviet Air Forces now serves with the air arms of Egypt, Iraq, Libya and Syria.

Notes: The MiG-23 is currently serving in three versions, these being the single-seat air superiority and air intercept MiG-23F (Flogger-B) with a 90-cm diameter radar, the MiG-23U (Flogger-C) tandem two-seat trainer which retains full operational capability and the MiG-23B (Flogger-D) which, illustrated on these pages, is intended for the battlefield interdiction and counterair roles and has a redesigned nose with laser seeker/ranger.

MIKOYAN MIG-23 (FLOGGER)

Dimensions: (Estimated) Span (max.), 46 ft 9 in (14,25 m), (min.), 26 ft 9½ in (8,17 m); length, 55 ft 1½ in (16,80 m); wing area, 293·4 sq ft (27,26 m²).

MIKOYAN MIG-25 (FOXBAT)

Country of Origin: USSR.

Type: Single-seat interceptor (Foxbat-A) and high-altitude reconnaissance aircraft (Foxbat-B).

Power Plant: Two (estimated) 16,755 lb (7 600 kg) dry and 24,250 lb (11 000 kg) reheat Tumansky turbofans.

Performance: (Estimated) Max. short-period dash speed, 2,100 mph (3 380 km/h) or Mach 3·2 at 39,370 ft (12 000 m); max. sustained speed, 1,780 mph (2 865 km/h) or Mach 2·7 at 39,370 ft (12 000 m); time to 36,090 ft (11 000 m), 2·5 min, (without reheat), 8·0 min; service ceiling, 72,180 ft (22 000 m); intercept radius, 620 mls (1 000 km); normal endurance, 3·5 hrs.

Weights: (Estimated) Empty equipped, 34,000 lb (15 420 kg); normal loaded, 50,000–55,000 lb (22 680–24 950 kg); max. take-off, 64,200 lb (29 120 kg).

Armament: (Foxbat-A) Two IR-homing and two semi-active radar-homing AA-6 AAMs on wing pylons.

Status: Believed flown in prototype form 1963–64 with service deliveries following from 1970–71.

Notes: The Foxbat-A interceptor version of the MiG-25 (illustrated) differs from the Foxbat-B reconnaissance model primarily in the nose section, the Jay Bird intercept radar being replaced by a camera installation. The MiG-25 has established a number of FAI-recognised records since 1965, the most recent, set up by a modified version (assigned the designation Ye-266M) with 30,865 lb (14 000 kg) engines in May 1975, were time-to-height records, altitudes of 82,021 ft (25 000m), 98,425 ft (30 000 m) and 114,829 ft (35 000 m) being attained in 154·2, 189·5 and 251·3 seconds. A training version with separate tandem cockpits is in service.

MIKOYAN MIG-25 (FOXBAT)

Dimensions: (Estimated) Span, 45 ft 0 in (13,70 m); length (including probe), 75 ft 0 in (22,86 m); height, 18 ft 0 in (5,50 m).

MITSUBISHI FS-T2 KAI

Country of Origin: Japan.

Type: Single-seat ground attack aircraft.

Power Plant: Two 3,820 lb (1 730 kg) and 7,070 lb (3 210 kg) reheat Ishikawajima-Harima TF40-IHI-801A (Rolls-Royce/Turboméca RB.172-T.260 Adour) turbofans.

Performance: Max. speed, 1,056 mph (1 700 km/h) at 40,000 ft (12 190 m) or Mach 1·6; combat radius (hi-lo-hi) with 12 500-lb (226,8-kg) bombs, 345 mls (555 km); max. ferry range, 1,785 mls (2 870 km); time to 36,090 ft (11 000 m), 2·0 min.

Weights: Empty equipped, 14,330 lb (6 500 kg); max. take-off, 30,200 lb (13 700 kg).

Armament: One 20-mm multi-barrel Vulcan M61A-1 cannon and up to 8,000 lb (3 629 kg) of stores on seven external stations (one under fuselage and six under wings). Two infrared homing AAMs may be mounted at wingtips. Typical load comprises eight 500-lb (226,8-kg) bombs plus two 183 Imp gal (832 l) fuel tanks. Primary weapon intended to be Mitsubishi ASM-1 anti-shipping missile.

Status: First prototype flown on June 7, 1975, having been preceded by second prototype which flew on June 3. Initial batch of 18 for delivery between September 1977 and March 1978 to Japanese Air Self-Defence Force, with further 50 programmed for delivery prior to March 1980.

Notes: The FS-T2 Kai is a single-seat ground attack variant of the T-2 tandem two-seat advanced trainer (see 1975 edition) from which it differs primarily in having the aft cockpit deleted, a passive warning radar antenna on top of the vertical tail surfaces, two additional wing hard points and a new fire control system.

MITSUBISHI FS-T2 KAI

Dimensions: Span, 25 ft 10 in (7,87 m); length, 58 ft 7 in (17,86 m); height, 14 ft 7 in (4,44 m); wing area, 228 sq ft (21,18 m²).

NORTHROP F-5E TIGER II

Country of Origin: USA.

Type: Single-seat air-superiority fighter.

Power Plant: Two 3,500 lb (1 588 kg) dry and 5,000 lb (2 268 kg) reheat General Electric J85-GE-21 turbojets.

Performance: Max. speed (at 13,220 lb/5 997 kg), 1056 mph (1 700 km/h) or Mach 1·6 at 36,090 ft (11 000 m), 760 mph (1 223 km/h) or Mach 1·0 at sea level, (with wingtip missiles), 990 mph (1 594 km/h) or Mach 1·5 at 36,090 ft (11 000 m); combat radius (internal fuel), 173 mls (278 km), (with 229 Imp gal/1 041 l drop tank), 426 mls (686 km); initial climb (at 13,220 lb/5 997 kg), 31,600 ft/min (160,53 m/sec); combat ceiling, 53,500 ft (16 305 m).

Weights: Take-off (wingtip launching rail configuration), 15,400 lb (6 985 kg); max. take-off, 24,083 lb (10 924 kg).

Armament: Two 20-mm M-39 cannon with 280 rpg and two wingtip-mounted AIM-9 Sidewinder AAMs. Up to 7,000 lb (3 175 kg) of ordnance (for attack role).

Status: First F-5E flown August 11, 1972, and first deliveries February 1973. Forty-eight delivered during 1973, followed by 158 in 1974, and some 250 in 1975, production tempo being 18 per month at the beginning of 1976.

Notes: A more powerful derivative of the F-5A (see 1970 edition) optimised for the air-superiority role, the F-5E won the USAF's International Fighter Aircraft (IFA) contest in November 1970, and is being supplied under the Military Assistance Programme to South Korea, Taiwan, Thailand and Jordan. Orders for the F-5E have also been placed by Brazil, Chile, Iran, Saudi Arabia and Malaysia. The first two-seat F-5F flew on September 25, 1974, and production deliveries of this version are scheduled to commence June 1976. The photo above depicts the F-5E fitted with the optional camera nose.

NORTHROP F-5E TIGER II

Dimensions: Span, 26 ft 8½ in (8,14 m); length, 48 ft 2½ in (14,69 m); height, 13 ft 4 in (4,06 m); wing area, 186·2 sq ft (17,29 m²).

NZAI CT-4 AIRTRAINER

Country of Origin: New Zealand.
Type: Side-by-side two-seat primary trainer.
Power Plant: One 210 hp Continental IO-360-H six-cylinder horizontally-opposed engine.
Performance: Max. speed, 183 mph (294 km/h) at sea level, 168 mph (270 km/h) at 10,000 ft (3 048 m); cruise (75% power), 158 mph (254 km/h) at sea level, 144 mph (232 km/h) at 10,000 ft (3 048 m), (55% power), 138 mph (222 km/h) at sea level; max. range (at 65% power), 824 mls (1 326 km) at 135 mph (217 km/h) at 5,000 ft (1 524 m), (with two 17·5 Imp gal/79,5 l wingtip tanks), 1,400 mls (2 253 km) at 5,000 ft (1 524 m); initial climb, 1,345 ft/min (6,8 m/sec).
Weights: Empty equipped, 1,520 lb (690 kg); design max. take-off, 2,400 lb (1 088 kg).
Status: Prototype flown February 21, 1972, with first production (to Royal Thai Air Force) October 1973. Deliveries to the RAAF were scheduled to be completed in March 1976.
Notes: Manufactured by New Zealand Aerospace Industries (NZAI) formed in 1973 by the amalgamation of Aero Engine Services and Air Parts (NZ), the CT-4 has been ordered by the Royal Thai Air Force (24), by the Royal Australian Air Force (37), by the Royal New Zealand Air Force (13) and by the Royal Hong Kong Auxiliary Air Force (three).

NZAI CT-4 AIRTRAINER

Dimensions: Span, 26 ft 0 in (7,92 m); length, 23 ft 2 in (7,06 m); height, 8 ft 6 in (2,59 m); wing area, 129 sq ft (12,00 m²).

PANAVIA MRCA

Countries of Origin: UK, Federal Germany and Italy.
Type: Two-seat multi-role fighter.
Power Plant: Two 8,500 lb (3 855 kg) dry and 14,500 lb (6 577 kg) reheat Turbo-Union RB.199-34R-2 turbofans.
Performance: (Estimated) Max. speed (clean), 840 mph (1 350 km/h) at 500 ft (150 m) or Mach 1·1, 1,385 mph (2 230 km/h) at 36,090 ft (11 000 m) or Mach 2·1; tactical radius (hi-lo-hi interdiction mission on internal fuel with typical external ordnance), 560 mls (900 km); service ceiling, 50,000 ft (15 250 m).
Weights: (Estimated) Empty equipped, 27,560 lb (12 500 kg); loaded (clean), 39,680 lb (18 000 kg); max. take-off, 50,705 lb (23 000 kg).
Armament: Two 27-mm Mauser cannon with 125 rpg and various ordnance combinations on seven (three fixed and four swivelling) stores stations.
Status: First of nine prototypes flown on August 14, 1974, and six prototypes flown (three in UK, two in Germany and one in Italy) by beginning of 1976. Prototypes to be followed by six pre-production aircraft and current planning calls for acquisition of 385 MRCAs by the RAF, 302 by Federal Germany (120 for the *Marineflieger* and 202 for the *Luftwaffe*) and approximately 100 by Italy for the *Aeronautica Militare*. Production deliveries scheduled to commence 1978.
Notes: The MRCA (multi-role combat aircraft) is being developed by Panavia, a multi-national European company, basically for the interdiction and strike roles, but an intercept version is projected for the RAF.

PANAVIA MRCA

Dimensions: Span (max.), 45 ft 7 in (13,90 m), (min.), 27 ft $5\frac{1}{8}$ in (8,36 m); length, (including probe), 56 ft $6\frac{1}{2}$ in (17,23 m); height, 18 ft 10 in (5,74 m).

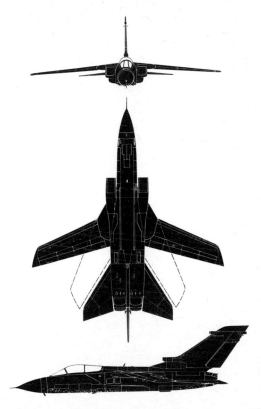

PIPER CHEROKEE ARCHER II

Country of Origin: USA.

Type: Light cabin monoplane.

Power Plant: One 180 hp Avco Lycoming O-360-A3A four-cylinder horizontally-opposed engine.

Performance: Max. cruise (75% power), 144 mph (233 km/h) at 7,000 ft (2 130 m); range at max. cruise (optimum altitude with max. fuel), 770 mls (1 239 km), at 65% power, 900 mls (1 448 km); initial climb, 740 ft/min (3,76 m/sec); service ceiling, 13,650 ft (4 160 m).

Weights: Empty equipped, 1,395 lb (633 kg); max. take-off, 2,450 lb (1 110 kg).

Accommodation: Four persons in pairs of individual seats. Dual controls.

Status: Archer II introduced in October 1975 to replace the Archer in the 1976 Cherokee range, production of which (all models) averaged some 120 per month during 1975.

Notes: The Archer II differs from the original Archer—introduced in October 1974 as successor to the similarly-powered Challenger in the Cherokee range (see 1973 edition)—primarily in having a tapered, longer-span wing first introduced by the Warrior (see 1974 edition). This increases both useful load and cruise speed by reducing induced drag. The Archer II is essentially similar to the Warrior apart from power plant, the latter having a 150 hp Avco Lycoming O-320-E3D, other Cherokee variants including the Arrow II which is similar to the original Archer apart from a retractable undercarriage and 200 hp IO-360-C1C engine.

172

PIPER CHEROKEE ARCHER II

Dimensions: Span, 35 ft 0 in (10,67 m); length, 24 ft 0 in (7,32 m); height, 7 ft 9¾ in (2,38 m); wing area, 170 sq ft (15,79 m²).

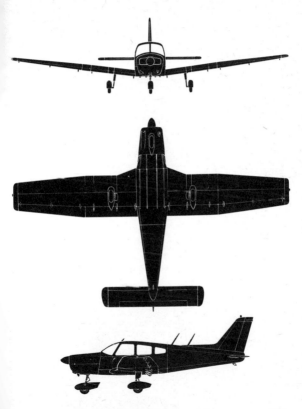

PIPER CHEROKEE LANCE

Country of Origin: USA.

Type: Light cabin monoplane.

Power Plant: One 300 hp Avco Lycoming IO-540-K1A5 six-cylinder horizontally-opposed engine.

Performance: Max. speed, 190 mph (306 km/h); max. cruise (75% power), 182 mph (293 km/h) at optimum altitude; range (75% power), 1,005 mls (1 618 km), (55% power), 1,120 mls (1 803 km); max. climb rate, 1,000 ft/min (5,08 m/sec); service ceiling, 14,600 ft (4 450 m).

Weights: Empty equipped, 1,910 lb (867 kg); max. take-off, 3,600 lb (1 633 kg).

Accommodation: Six persons in pairs with optional seventh seat between two centre seats. Dual controls standard.

Status: Prototype flown in August 1974, with customer deliveries commencing October 1975.

Notes: Featuring an essentially similar fuselage to that of the Seneca II which, in turn, is a twin-engined derivative of the Cherokee Six, the Cherokee Lance has a similar retractable undercarriage to that of the Seneca II and an identical four-tank fuel system, and is produced on a common production line with the Seneca and Cherokee Six. The last-mentioned type, which is produced in two versions, the Cherokee Six 260 and 300 with 260 and 300 hp engines respectively, differs from the Cherokee Lance principally in having a fixed nosewheel undercarriage and a two-tank fuel system with auxiliary tanks in the glassfibre wingtips. Production of the Cherokee Six averaged 17–18 per month during 1975.

PIPER CHEROKEE LANCE

Dimensions: Span, 32 ft 9½ in (9,99 m); length, 27 ft 8¾ in (8,45 m); height, 7 ft 11 in (2,41 m); wing area, 174·5 sq ft (16,21 m²).

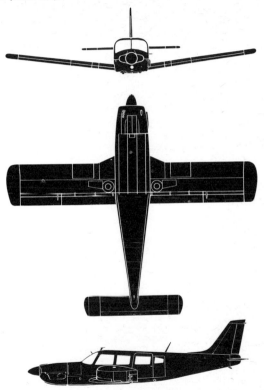

PZL-106 KRUK

Country of Origin: Poland.

Type: Single-seat agricultural monoplane.

Power Plant: One 600 hp PZL-3S (LIT-3S) seven-cylinder radial air-cooled engine.

Performance: (Production) Max. speed, 137 mph (220 km/h) at 6,560 ft (2 000 m); max. cruise, 112 mph (180 km/h); operating speed (with 2,204-lb/1 000-kg chemical load), 75–99 mph (120–160 km/h).

Weights: (Production) Empty, 3,527 lb (1 600 kg); max. take-off, 6,614 lb (3 000 kg).

Status: First prototype flown on April 17, 1973, followed by second in October 1973 and third in October 1974. Series production scheduled to commence during 1976.

Notes: First and second prototypes powered by Avco Lycoming IO-720-A1B eight-cylinder horizontally-opposed engine and third prototype by PZL-3S radial. First prototype fitted with wooden wings, but all subsequent aircraft have metal wings. The production model, which will standardise on the PZL-3S engine, differs from the prototypes in having a 5·49-ft (1,8-m) increase in wing span, resulting in a 41·23 sq ft (3,83 m²) increase in gross wing area. Nine degrees of wing sweep were introduced after initial flight testing. Production of at least 600 Kruk (Raven) agricultural monoplanes for the member countries of the CMEA (Council for Mutual Economic Aid) is anticipated.

PZL-106 KRUK

Dimensions: (Production) Span, 48 ft 6⅔ in (14,80 m); length, 29 ft 2½ in (8,90 m); height, 9 ft 6¼ in (2,90 m); wing area, 359·51 sq ft (33,40 m²).

ROCKWELL COMMANDER 114

Country of Origin: USA.

Type: Light cabin monoplane.

Power Plant: One 260 hp Avco Lycoming IO-540-T4A5D six-cylinder horizontally-opposed engine.

Performance: Max. speed, 185 mph (298 km/h) at sea level; cruise at 75% power at optimum altitude, 180 mph (290 km/h); range (including 45 min reserve at 45% power), 720 mls (1 158 km) at 75% power, 820 mls (1 319 km) at 55% power; initial climb, 1,054 ft/min (5,35 m/sec); service ceiling, 16,800 ft (5 120 m).

Weights: Empty, 1,790 lb (812 kg); max. take-off, 3,140 lb (1 424 kg).

Accommodation: Pilot and three passengers seated in pairs with individual seats forward and bench seat aft.

Status: Commander 114 introduced November 1975 with initial customer deliveries early 1976. Derived from and manufactured in parallel with Model 112A, deliveries of which averaged 15–16 monthly during 1975. Model 112A introduced January 1974 as successor to Model 112 of which customer deliveries commenced late 1972.

Notes: The Commander 114 differs from the Commander 112A (see 1975 edition) primarily in the engine installed, the latter having a 200 hp IO-360-C1D6. The Commander 112TC introduced simultaneously with the 114 has a 210 hp turbosupercharged TO-360-C1A6D engine and extended wings increasing overall span to 35 ft 7⅝ in (10,86 m).

ROCKWELL COMMANDER 114

Dimensions: Span, 32 ft 9 in (9,98 m); length, 24 ft 10 in (7,57 m); height, 8 ft 5 in (2,56 m); wing area, 152 sq ft (14,12 m²).

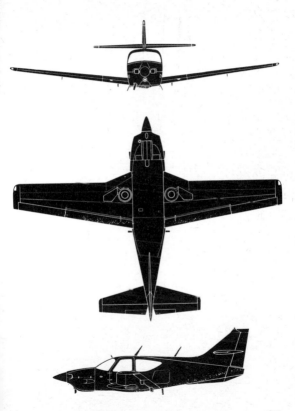

ROCKWELL INTERNATIONAL B-1

Country of Origin: USA.

Type: Strategic heavy bomber.

Power Plant: Four 17,000 lb (7 711 kg) dry and 30,000 lb (13 608 kg) reheat General Electric F101-GE-100 turbofans.

Performance: (Prototypes estimated) Max. speed, 1,450 mph (2 334 km/h) at 40,000 ft (12 190 m) or Mach 2·2, 900 mph (1 450 km/h) at 1,500 ft (460 m) or Mach 1·2, 648 mph (1 042 km/h) at sea level or Mach 0·85; max. range (internal fuel), 6,100 mls (9 820 km).

Weights: Max. take-off (design), 389,800 lb (176 822 kg).

Armament: Twenty-four Boeing AGM-69A SRAM (Short-Range Attack Missile) ASMs in three weapons bays, plus eight SRAMs on four underfuselage hardpoints. Max. permissible weapons load, 115,000 lb (52 160 kg).

Status: First of four prototypes flown December 23, 1974, with second and third scheduled to fly in June and March 1976 respectively and fourth to fly in February 1979. Production decision scheduled for November 1976. USAF hopes to order 240 production B-1As.

Notes: The first three prototypes feature crew escape modules which, together with the planned variable-geometry engine intakes, are being deleted from later aircraft as economy measures. The fourth prototype will have separate ejection seats for the crew members, lighter nacelle intake structure, lighter wing carry-through structure and other changes to reduce structural weight by at least 10,000 lb (4 540 kg). The fixed intake geometry will result in a reduction of Mach 0·6 in the maximum attainable speed of the B-1A. The third prototype is to be equipped with the full avionics system.

ROCKWELL INTERNATIONAL B-1

Dimensions: Span (max.), 136 ft 8½ in (41,66 m), (min.),
78 ft 2½ in (23,83 m); length (including probe), 150 ft 2½ in
(45,80 m); height, 33 ft 7¼ in (10,24 m); wing area (approx.),
1,950 sq ft (181,2 m²).

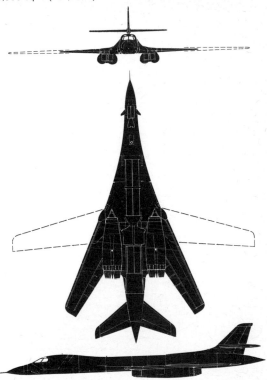

SAAB SUPPORTER

Country of Origin: Sweden.

Type: Two-seat primary trainer, forward air control and light close support aircraft.

Power Plant: One 200 hp Avco Lycoming IO-360-A1B6 four-cylinder horizontally-opposed engine.

Performance: Max. speed (at 1,984 lb/900 kg), 155 mph (250 km/h) at sea level, (at 2,425 lb/1 100 kg), 153 mph (246 km/h); cruise at 75% power (at 1,984 lb/900 kg), 138 mph (222 km/h) at sea level; range (clean aircraft with 10% reserves), 580 mls (933 km) at 130 mph (209 km/h) at sea level; initial climb (at 2,204 lb/1 000 kg), 1,082 ft/min (5,5 m/sec).

Weights: Empty, 1,415 lb (642 kg); max. take-off, 2,425 lb (1 100 kg).

Armament (Close support role) Six underwing hardpoints of which two inboard stressed for 330-lb (150-kg) loads and remainder for 220-lb (100-kg) loads. Max. weight of ordnance (including pylons) is 661 lb (300 kg), typical loads including six Bofors anti-tank missiles, 18 75-mm Bofors rockets, two 7,62-mm gun pods, or four Abel pods each with seven 68-mm rockets.

Status: Prototype flown (as MFI 15) on July 11, 1969, with first of 12 pre-production (Safari/Supporter) aircraft following on April 9, 1973. Initial production batch of 65 begun July 1974 with deliveries commencing February 1975.

Notes: Safari (originally MFI 15) is civil equivalent of Supporter (originally MFI 17), 45 of the latter having been ordered by Pakistan and a further 32 by Denmark.

SAAB SUPPORTER

Dimensions: Span, 29 ft 0½ in (8,85 m); length, 22 ft 11½ in (7,00 m); height, 8 ft 6¼ in (2,60 m); wing area, 128·09 sq ft (11,90 m²).

SAAB (JA) 37 VIGGEN

Country of Origin: Sweden.

Type: Single-seat all-weather intercepter fighter with secondary strike capability.

Power Plant: One 16,203 lb (7 350 kg) dry and 28,108 lb (12 750 kg) reheat Volvo Flygmotor RM 8B.

Performance: (Estimated) Max. speed (with two RB 24 Sidewinder AAMs), 1,320 mph (2 125 km/h) above 36,090 ft (11 000 m) or Mach 2·0, 910 mph (1 465 km/h) at 1,000 ft (305 m) or Mach 1·2; operational radius (M = 2·0 intercept with two AAMs), 250 mls (400 km), (lo-lo-lo ground attack with six Mk. 82 bombs), 300 mls (480 km); time (from brakes off) to 32,810 ft (10 000 m), 1·4 min.

Weights: (Estimated) Empty, 26,895 lb (12 200 kg); loaded (two AAMs), 37,040 lb (16 800 kg); max. take-off, 49,600 lb (22 500 kg).

Armament: One semi-externally mounted 30-mm Oerlikon KCA cannon with 150 rounds and up to 13,227 lb (6 000 kg) of ordnance on seven (three fuselage and four wing) external stores stations.

Status: First of four JA 37 prototypes (modified from AJ 37 airframes) flown June 1974, with fifth prototype built from outset to JA 37 standards. Initial production contract for 30 JA 37 Viggens placed late 1974 against anticipated procurement of 150–200 aircraft to re-equip eight interceptor squadrons commencing 1978.

Notes: The JA 37 is a development of the AJ 37 (see 1973 edition) which is optimised for the attack role, the SF 37 (see 1974 edition) and SH 37 being respectively tactical reconnaissance and sea surveillance derivatives of the latter. The JA 37 has uprated turbofan, cannon armament and X-Band Pulse Doppler radar.

SAAB (JA) 37 VIGGEN

Dimensions: Span, 34 ft 9¼ in (10,60 m); length (excluding probe), 50 ft 8¼ in (15,45 m); height, 19 ft 4¼ in (5,90 m); wing area (including foreplanes), 561·88 sq ft (52,20 m²).

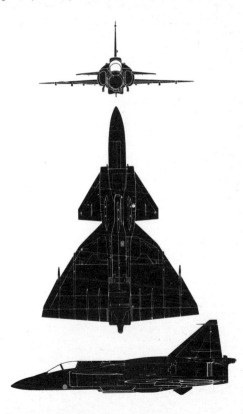

SCOTTISH AVIATION BULLDOG 200

Country of Origin: United Kingdom.

Type: Four-seat multi-purpose light military aircraft.

Power Plant: One 200 hp Avco Lycoming IO-360-A1B6 four-cylinder horizontally-opposed engine.

Performance: (Estimated) Max. speed, 173 mph (278 km/h) at sea level; cruise at 75% power, 162 mph (261 km/h) at 4,000 ft (1 220 m); max. fuel range (at 55% power), 680 mls (1 094 km); max. endurance, 5 hrs; initial climb, 1,160 ft/min (5,9 m/sec); service ceiling, 18,500 ft (5 639 m).

Weights: Typical empty operational, 1,810 lb (820 kg); max. aerobatic, 2,293 lb (1 040 kg); max. take-off, 2,601 lb (1 180 kg).

Armament: (Light strike role and weapons training) Four wing hardpoints with combined maximum capacity of 640 lb (290 kg) of ordnance.

Status: Prototype (the 258th Bulldog airframe) scheduled to fly during May 1976 with production deliveries commencing in 1977.

Notes: The Bulldog 200 is a progressive development of the fixed-gear Bulldog 120 (see 1974 edition) which is intended to complement but not replace the earlier model. Suitable for use as a weapons trainer, for light strike duties, for basic and aerobatic training, for liaison and tactical reconnaissance, and other military roles, the Bulldog 200 has a fully retractable undercarriage, provision for a fourth seat in the cockpit, a lengthened and cleaner engine cowling, a repositioned fire-wall and a "plug" type canopy of revised contour. First 98 production Bulldogs were of the Series 100 version, this being succeeded by the Series 120 embodying minor improvements and currently in production.

SCOTTISH AVIATION BULLDOG 200

Dimensions: Span, 33 ft 0 in (10,06 m); length, 22 ft 3 in (7,08 m); height, 7 ft 5¾ in (2,28 m); wing area, 129·4 sq ft (12,02 m²).

SEPECAT JAGUAR G.R. MK. 1

Countries of Origin: France and United Kingdom.
Type: Single-seat tactical strike fighter.
Power Plant: Two 4,620 lb (2 100 kg) dry and 7,140 lb (3 240 kg) reheat Rolls-Royce Turboméca RT.172 Adour 102 turbofans.
Performance: (At typical weight) Max. speed, 820 mph (1 320 km/h) or Mach 1·1 at 1,000 ft (305 m), 1,057 mph (1 700 km/h) or Mach 1·6 at 32,810 ft (10 000 m); cruise with max. ordnance, 430 mph (690 km/h) or Mach 0·65 at 39,370 ft (12 000 m); range with external fuel for lo-lo-lo mission profile, 450 mls (724 km), for hi-lo-hi mission profile, 710 mls (1 142 km); ferry range, 2,270 mls (3 650 km).
Weights: Normal take-off, 23,000 lb (10 430 kg); max. take-off, 32,600 lb (14 790 kg).
Armament: Two 30-mm Aden cannon and up to 10,000 lb (4 536 kg) ordnance on five external hardpoints.
Status: First of eight prototypes flown September 8, 1968. First production Jaguar E for France flown November 2, 1971, with first Jaguar A following April 20, 1972. First production Jaguar S for UK flown October 11, 1972. By the beginning of 1976, France had ordered 180 Jaguars and the UK had ordered 202.
Notes: Both France and UK have a requirement for approximately 200 Jaguars, French versions being the single-seat A (*Appui Tactique*) and two-seat E (*École de Combat*), and British versions being the single-seat S (G.R. Mk. 1) and the two-seat B (T Mk. 2). The G.R. Mk. 1 differs from the Jaguar A in having a nose-mounted laser rangefinder and tail-mounted avionics pack. The export Jaguar International with uprated Adour 804 engines has been ordered by Oman (12) and Ecuador (12).

SEPECAT JAGUAR G.R. MK. 1

Dimensions: Span, 28 ft 6 in (8,69 m); length, 50 ft 11 in (15,52 m); height, 16 ft 0½ in (4,89 m); wing area, 260·3 sq ft (24,18 m²).

SHINMEIWA US-1

Country of Origin: Japan.

Type: Amphibious search and rescue flying boat.

Power Plant: Four 3,060 ehp Ishikawajima-Harima-built General Electric T64-IHI-10 turboprops.

Performance: Max. speed, 299 mph (481 km/h) at 9,840 ft (3 000 m); high-speed cruise, 265 mph (426 km/h) at 9,840 ft (3 000 m); long-range cruise (two engines), 202 mph (325 km/h) at 8,200 ft (2 500 m); loiter speed, 161 mph (259 km/h) at 1,000 ft (305 m); search endurance, 6 hrs at 690-mile (1 110 km) range; max. search and rescue range, 3,145 mls (5 060 km); initial climb, 2,360 ft/min (12,0 m/sec); service ceiling, 28,000 ft (8 535 m).

Weights: Empty equipped, 56,218 lb (25 500 kg); max. take-off, 99,208 lb (45 000 kg).

Accommodation: Crew of eight comprising pilot, co-pilot, flight engineer, radar operator, navigator, radio operator, observer and rescue man. Up to five medical attendants and 36 stretcher casualties.

Status: First of three US-1s ordered by the Japanese Maritime Self-Defence Force flown October 16, 1974, and delivered March 1975, with second and third aircraft following in June and December respectively. Development continuing.

Notes: The US-1 (alias SS-2A) is an amphibious rescue derivative of the SS-2 maritime patrol flying boat (see 1974 edition). Featuring a retractable undercarriage, the main twinwheel members of which retract into bulged housings, the US-1 has a 1,400 ehp General Electric T58-10 turboshaft driving a boundary-layer control compressor for the flaps, elevators and rudder.

190

SHINMEIWA US-1

Dimensions: Span, 107 ft 6½ in (32,78 m); length, 109 ft 11 in (33,50 m); height, 32 ft 3 in (9,83 m); wing area, 1,453·13 sq ft (135,00 m²).

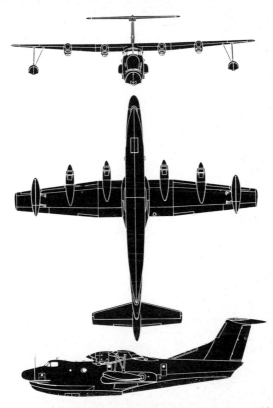

SHORTS SD3-30

Country of Origin: United Kingdom.

Type: Third-level airliner and utility transport.

Power Plant: Two 1,120 shp Pratt & Whitney (Canada) PT6A-45 turboprops.

Performance: (At 20,000 lb/9 072 kg) Max. cruise, 227 mph (365 km/h) at 10,000 ft (3 050 m); econ. cruise, 184 mph (297 km/h) at 10,000 ft (3 050 m); range (no reserves) with 30 passengers and baggage (5,940 lb/2 694 kg), 500 mls (800 km); ferry range, 1,150 mls (1 850 km); max. climb, 1,210 ft/min (6,14 m/sec).

Weights: Empty equipped (for 30 passengers), 14,200 lb (6 441 kg); max. take-off, 22,000 lb (9 979 kg).

Accommodation: Standard flight crew of two and normal accommodation for 30 passengers in 10 rows three abreast and 1,000 lb (455 kg) of baggage.

Status: Engineering prototype flown August 22, 1974, with production prototype following on July 8, 1975. First production aircraft flown in December 1975, with third being first customer delivery example. Orders by beginning of 1976 included three for Command Airways and three for Times Air. Maximum anticipated production rate of four per month.

Notes: Intended primarily for commuter and regional air service operators, the SD3-30 is also being offered for the military tactical transport role as the SD3-M, other missions including coastal patrol and reconnaissance, casualty evacuation, search and rescue, and aerial survey. The SD3-M will accommodate 31 fully-equipped paratroops and will feature a large rear-loading door.

SHORTS SD3-30

Dimensions: Span, 74 ft 8 in (22,76 m); length, 58 ft 0½ in (17,69 m); height, 16 ft 3 in (4,95 m); wing area, 453 sq ft (42,10 m²).

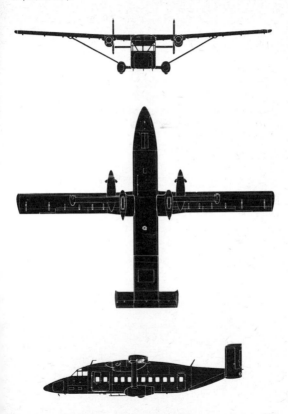

SIAI-MARCHETTI SM.1019E

Country of Origin: Italy.

Type: Battlefield surveillance and forward air control aircraft.

Power Plant: One 400 shp Allison 250-B17 turboprop.

Performance: Max. speed, 181 mph (287 km/h) at sea level; max. cruise (75% power), 146 mph (235 km/h) at sea level, 149 mph (239 km/h) at 9,850 ft (3 000 m); max. range, 702 mls (1 130 km) at sea level, 832 mls (1 340 km) at 10,000 ft (3 050 m); initial climb, 1,319 ft/min (6,7 m/sec); service ceiling, 21,325 ft (6 500 m).

Weights: Empty equipped, 1,521 lb (690 kg); max. take-off, 3,196 lb (1 450 kg).

Armament: Two stores stations under wings capable of carrying Minigun pods, rockets, etc, up to a maximum external load of 500 lb (227 kg).

Status: First prototype flown May 24, 1969, with second prototype (SM.1019A) following on February 18, 1971. Deliveries of initial production batch of 40 (SM.1019E) begun mid-1975 against total Italian Army requirement of 100 aircraft programmed for completion by end of 1976.

Notes: The SM.1019 is based upon the Cessna O-1 Bird Dog but possesses an extensively modified airframe to meet latest operational requirements, redesigned tail surfaces and a turboprop in place of the O-1's piston engine. Whereas the second prototype, the SM.1019A (see 1975 edition), had a 317 shp Allison 250-B15G turboprop, the more powerful 250-B17 has been standardised for the production SM.1019E. The pilot and co-pilot or observer/systems operator are seated in tandem and dual controls are optional.

SIAI-MARCHETTI SM.1019E

Dimensions: Span, 36 ft 0 in (10,97 m); length, 27 ft 10⅔ in (8,52 m); height, 9 ft 4½ in (2,86 m); wing area, 173·94 sq ft (16,16 m²).

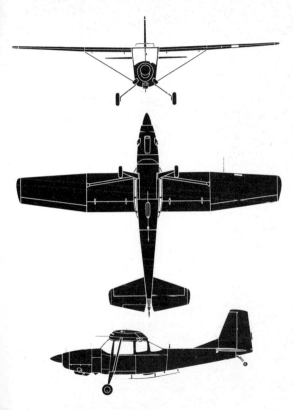

SUKHOI SU-17 (FITTER-C)

Country of Origin: USSR.

Type: Single-seat tactical strike fighter.

Power Plant: One 17,195 lb (7 800 kg) dry and 24,700 lb (11 200 kg) reheat Lyulka AL-21F-3 turbojet.

Performance: Max. speed (clean), 808 mph (1 300 km/h) or Mach 1·06 at sea level, 1,430 mph (2 300 km/h) at 39,370 ft (12 000 m) or Mach 2·17; combat radius (lo-lo-lo mission profile), 260 mls (420 km), (hi-lo-hi mission profile), 373 mls (600 km); range (with 2,205-lb/1 000-kg weapon load and auxiliary fuel), 1,415 mls (2 280 km); service ceiling, 57,415 ft (17 500 m).

Weights: Max. take-off, 39,022 lb (17 700 kg).

Armament: Two 30-mm NR-30 cannon with 70 rpg and (for short-range missions) a max. external ordnance load of 7,716 lb (3 500 kg). Typical external stores include UV-16-57 or UV-32-57 rocket pods containing 16 and 32 55-mm S-5 rockets respectively, 240-mm S-24 rockets, two AS-7 Kerry ASMs, or 550-lb (250-kg) or 1,100-lb (500-kg) bombs.

Status: The Su-17 entered service with the Soviet Air Forces in 1972, and is currently being exported to Warsaw Pact countries, having entered service with the Polish Air Force during the course of 1974.

Notes: The Su-17 is a variable-geometry derivative of the Su-7 Fitter-A (see 1973 edition), a variable-geometry technology demonstration version of which (Fitter-B) was first seen at Domodedovo in July 1967. Intended primarily for the close air support, battlefield interdiction and counterair roles, but with secondary combat zone air superiority capability, the Su-17 has apparently been offered for export (eg, to India) under the designation Su-20.

SUKHOI SU-17 (FITTER-C)

Estimated Dimensions: Span (max.), 45 ft 0 in (13,70 m), (min.), 32 ft 6 in (9,90 m); length (including probe), 57 ft 0 in (17,37 m); height, 15 ft 5 in (4,70 m).

SUKHOI SU-19 (FENCER-A)

Country of Origin: USSR.

Type: Two-seat ground attack fighter.

Power Plant: Two (estimated) 13,230 lb (6 000 kg) dry and 19,840 lb (9 000 kg) reheat turbojets.

Performance: (Estimated) Max. speed, 760–840 mph (1 225–1 350 km/h) at sea level or Mach 1·0–1·1, 1,385–1,520 mph (2 230–2 445 km/h) at 36,090 ft (11 000 m) or Mach 2·1–2·3; radius of action (lo-lo-lo), 250 mls (400 km), (hi-lo-hi), 750 mls (1 200 km); max. endurance, 3–4 hrs.

Weights: (Estimated) Empty equipped, 33,000 lb (14 970 kg); max. take-off, 68,000 lb (30 845 kg).

Armament: One six-barrel 23-mm rotary cannon in the underside of the fuselage and up to 10,000–11,000 lb (4 500–5 000 kg) of ordnance on six external stations (two under the fuselage and four under the fixed wing glove), a typical ordnance load comprising two 1,100-lb (500-kg) bombs, two surface-to-air missiles and two pods each containing 16 or 32 57-mm unguided rockets.

Status: Prototypes of the Su-19 are believed to have flown in 1970, and this type was first reported to be in service with the Soviet Air Forces during the course of 1974. Western intelligence agencies indicated that several hundred were expected to have attained service by mid-1976.

Notes: The Su-19 (the accompanying illustrations of which should be considered as provisional) is the first Soviet fighter optimised for the ground attack role to have achieved service status. Wing leading-edge sweep varies from approximately 23 deg fully spread to 70 deg fully swept, and the wings reportedly incorporate both leading- and trailing-edge lift devices and lift dumpers acting as spoilers in conjunction with differential tailplane movement for roll control.

SUKHOI SU-19 (FENCER-A)

Dimensions: (Estimated): Span (max.), 56 ft (17,00 m), (min.), 31 ft (9,45 m); length, 70 ft (21,35 m).

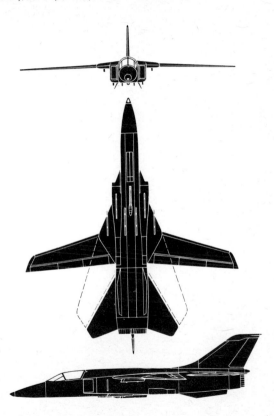

TUPOLEV (BACKFIRE-B)

Country of Origin: USSR.
Type: Strategic bomber.
Power Plant: Two (estimated) 33,070 lb (15 000 kg) dry and 46,300 lb (21 000 kg) reheat Kuznetsov turbofans.
Performance: (Estimated) Max. speed, 685 mph (1 100 km/h) or Mach 0·9 at sea level, 1,320 mph (2 125 km/h) at 39,370 ft (12 000 m); optimum cruise at altitude, 560 mph (900 km/h) or Mach 0·85; combat radius (lo-lo-lo), 1,240 mls (2 000 km), (hi-lo-hi), 2,485 mls (4 000 km), (hi-hi-hi), 3,730 mls (6 000 km); service ceiling, 59,000 ft (18 000 m).
Weights: (Estimated) Empty equipped, 121,255 lb (55 000 kg); max. take-off, 275,600 lb (125 000 kg).
Armament: (Estimated) Internal bomb load of up to 16,000 lb (7 250 kg) or two externally-mounted 9,920-lb (4 500-kg) AS-6 stand-off missiles with (approx.) 460-mile (740-km) range and inertial guidance.
Status: First reported in prototype form in 1969, the Backfire began to enter service with both the Soviet long-range aviation component and the Naval Air Force during the course of 1974, some 30 allegedly being in service by the beginning of 1976.
Notes: Backfire-B, provisional illustrations of which appear on these pages, is believed to be the production version of this strategic bomber, the pre-production variant being Backfire-A.

TUPOLEV (BACKFIRE-B)

Dimensions: (Estimated) Span (max.), 115 ft 0 in (35,00 m), (min.), 92 ft 0 in (28,00 m); length, 138 ft 0 in (42,00 m).

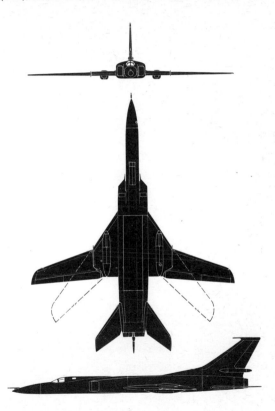

TUPOLEV TU-22 (BLINDER)

Country of Origin: USSR.
Type: Medium bomber and strike-reconnaissance aircraft.
Power Plant: Two (approx.) 15,000 lb (6 800 kg) dry and 27,000 lb (12 250 kg) reheat turbojets.
Performance: (Estimated) Max. speed (clean), 860 mph (1 385 km/h) at 36,090 ft (11 000 m) or Mach 1·3, 685 mph (1 100 km/h) at 1,000 ft (300 m) or Mach 0·9; tactical radius (hi-lo-hi), 1,370 mls (2 200 km) at 530 mph (850 km/h) or Mach 0·8.
Weights: Max. take-off (estimated), 185,000 lb (84 000 kg).
Armament: Internally-housed free-falling weapons or (Blinder-B) semi-recessed AS-4 Kitchen stand-off missile. Remotely-controlled 23-mm cannon in tail barbette.
Status: Believed to have attained operational status with the Soviet Air Forces in 1965. Limited production believed continuing into 1976.
Notes: Variants include (Blinder-A) standard bomber and strike aircraft and (Blinder-B) its missile-carrying version, (Blinder-C) a maritime reconnaissance model, (Blinder-D) an operational trainer, and a long-range heavy interceptor for periphery defence.

TUPOLEV TU-22 (BLINDER)

Dimensions: (Estimated) Span, 91 ft 0 in (27,74 m); length, 133 ft 0 in (40,50 m); height, 17 ft 0 in (5,18 m); wing area, 2,030 sq ft (188,59 m²).

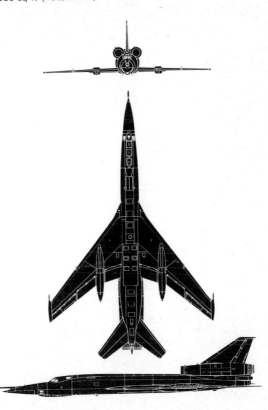

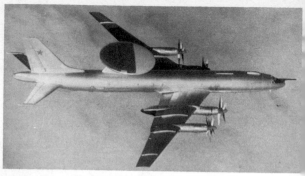

TUPOLEV TU-126 (MOSS)

Country of Origin: USSR.

Type: Airborne warning and control system aircraft.

Power Plant: Four 14,795 ehp Kuznetsov NK-12MV turbo-props.

Performance: (Estimated) Max. speed, 510 mph (820 km/h); max. continuous cruise, 460 mph (740 km/h) at 25,000 ft (7 620 m); operational cruise, 410 mph (660 km/h) at 21,325 ft (6 500 m); mission endurance (unrefuelled), 9 hrs at 620-mile (1 000-km) radius, 6 hrs at 1,240-mile (2 000-km) radius; service ceiling, 36,090 ft (11 000 m).

Weights: (Estimated) Normal max. take-off, 360,000 lb (163,290 kg).

Status: The Tu-126 AWACS aircraft is believed to have flown in prototype form in 1962–63 and first appeared in service with the Soviet Air Forces in the late 'sixties. Some 20–30 aircraft of this type are believed to be in service.

Notes: Essentially an adaptation of the Tu-114 commercial transport and retaining basically similar wings, tail surfaces power plant and undercarriage to those of the earlier aircraft, the Tu-126 is primarily intended to locate low-flying intruders and to vector interceptors towards them. The dominating feature of the aircraft is its pylon-mounted saucer-shaped early-warning scanner. The Tu-126 reportedly operates most effectively over water, possessing only limited overland "look-down" capability.

TUPOLEV TU-126 (MOSS)

Dimensions: Span, 168 ft 0 in (51,20 m); approx. length, 188 ft 0 in (57,30 m); height, 51 ft 0 in (15,50 m); wing area, 3,349 sq ft (311,1 m²).

TUPOLEV TU-134A (CRUSTY)

Country of Origin: USSR.

Type: Short- to medium-range commercial transport.

Power Plant: Two 14,990 lb (6 800 kg) Soloviev D-30-2 Turbofans.

Performance: Max. cruise, 528 mph (850 km/h) at 32,810 ft (10 000 m); long-range cruise, 466 mph (750 km/h) at 32,810 ft (10 000 m); max. range at long-range cruise with 1 hr reserves and 18,108-lb (8 215-kg) payload, 1,243 mls (2 000 km), with 8,818-lb (4 000-kg) payload, 2,175 mls (3 500 km).

Weights: Operational empty, 63,934 lb (29 000 kg); max. take-off, 103,617 lb (47 000 kg).

Accommodation: Basic flight crew of three and maximum of 80 passengers in four-abreast all-tourist class configuration.

Status: Prototype Tu-134A flown in 1968 and first production deliveries (to *Aeroflot*) mid-1970. Series production continuing at Kharkov at the beginning of 1976.

Notes: The Tu-134A differs from the original Tu-134, which entered *Aeroflot* service in 1966, in having an additional 6 ft 10⅔ in (2,10 m) section inserted in the fuselage immediately forward of the wing to permit two additional rows of passenger seats, and introduces engine thrust reversers. Maximum take-off weight has been increased by 5,512 lb (2 500 kg), maximum payload being raised by 1,025 lb (465 kg), an APU is provided, and radio and navigational equipment have been revised. Route proving trials with the Tu-134A were completed by *Aeroflot* late in 1970, and this airliner was introduced on international routes early in 1971. The shorter-fuselage Tu-134 serves with Aeroflot, CSA, Interflug, LOT, Malev, Bulair, Balkan-Bulgarian and Aviogenex.

TUPOLEV TU-134A (CRUSTY)

Dimensions: Span, 95 ft 2 in (29,00 m); length, 111 ft 0½ in (36,40 m); height, 29 ft 7 in (9,02 m); wing area, 1,370·3 sq ft (127,3 m²).

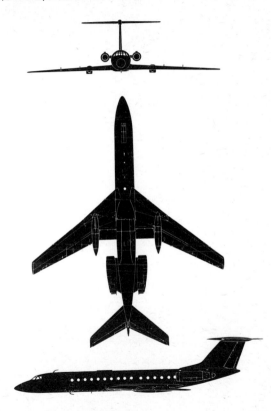

TUPOLEV TU-144 (CHARGER)

Country of Origin: USSR.

Type: Long-range supersonic commercial transport.

Power Plant: Four 33,100 lb (15 000 kg) dry and 44,000 lb (20 000 kg) reheat Kuznetsov NK-144 turbofans.

Performance: Max. cruise, 1,550 mph (2 500 km/h) or Mach 2·3 at altitudes up to 59,000 ft (18 000 m); subsonic cruise, 614 mph (988 km/h) or Mach 0·93 at 37,730 ft (11 500 m); range (with full payload), 4,000 mls (6 440 km); cruising altitude, 52,500 ft (16 460 m) to 59,000 ft (18 000 m).

Weights: Typical operational empty, 187,395 lb (85 000 kg); max. take-off, 396,830 lb (180 000 kg).

Accommodation: Basic flight crew of three and maximum of up to 140 passengers in single-class arrangement with three-plus-two and two-plus-two seating.

Status: First pre-production aircraft (representative of the production configuration) flown September 1971, and six aircraft of production standard had flown by mid-1975 when a further 12 were under construction against an anticipated Aeroflot requirement for approximately 30 aircraft. Scheduled service (freight only) between Moscow and Alma Ata begun December 26, 1975, and initial passenger services are expected to be flown during 1976.

Notes: The production-standard Tu-144 described and illustrated on these pages shares little more than a generally similar configuration with the prototype to which this designation was first applied and which flew for the first time on December 31, 1968. The current model has been lengthened by 20 ft 8 in (6,30 m) and the compound delta wing is of 3 ft 9 in (1,15 m) greater span than the ogee wing of the original aircraft.

TUPOLEV TU-144 (CHARGER)

Dimensions: Span, 94 ft 6 in (28,80 m); length, 215 ft 6½ in (65,70 m); height, 42 ft 3 in (12,85 m); wing area, 4,720 sq ft (438 m²).

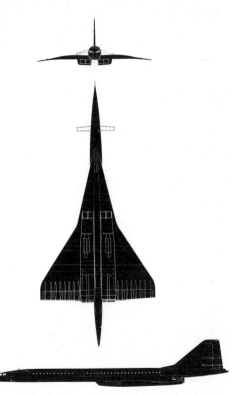

TUPOLEV TU-154A (CARELESS)

Country of Origin: USSR.

Type: Medium- to long-haul commercial transport.

Power Plant: Three 22,050 lb (10 000 kg) Kuznetsov NK-8-2U turbofans.

Performance: Max. cruise, 590 mph (950 km/h) at 31,170 ft (9 500 m); econ. cruise, 559 mph (900 km/h); range (with normal reserves and 39,683-lb/18 000-kg payload), 1,864 mls (3 000 km), (with 35,274-lb/16 000-kg payload), 2,050 mls (3 300 km), (with 27,557-lb/12 500-kg payload), 2,485 mls (4 000 km).

Weights: Max. take-off, 207,235 lb (94 00 kg).

Accommodation: Flight crew of three–four and basic arrangements for 152 or 168 passengers in six-abreast seating.

Status: Developed from the original Tu-154 (which flew as a prototype on October 4, 1968), the Tu-154A first flew late 1973 and entered Aeroflot service during April 1974.

Notes: The principal difference between the Tu-154A and the original Tu-154 (see 1975 edition) is the use of uprated engines which permit an 8,818-lb (4 000-kg) increase in max. take-off weight. An extra fuel tank is installed in the centre section. The Tu-154A can operate from airfields with category B surfaces, including packed earth and gravel. Operators of the earlier Tu-154 (which the Tu-154A has replaced in production) include Balkan-Bulgarian and Malev of Hungary. A version with stretched fuselage has been referred to as Tu-154M.

TUPOLEV TU-154A (CARELESS)

Dimensions: Span, 123 ft 2½ in (37,55 m); length, 157 ft 1¾ in (47,90 m); height, 37 ft 4¾ in (11,40 m); wing area, 2,168·92 sq ft (201,45 m²).

VALMET LEKO-70

Country of Origin: Finland.

Type: Side-by-side two-seat primary trainer.

Power Plant: One 200 hp Avco Lycoming IO-360-A1B6 four-cylinder horizontally-opposed engine.

Performance: Max. speed, 149 mph (240 km/h) at sea level; max. initial climb, 1,180 ft/min (6,0 m/sec). No further details available for publication.

Weights: Empty equipped (prototype), 1,587 lb (720 kg), (production), 1,521 lb (690 kg); max. take-off, 2,535 lb (1 150 kg).

Status: Prototype flown July 1, 1975, with production expected to commence during the course of 1976 against a Finnish Air Force requirement for 30 aircraft.

Notes: Intended to succeed the Saab 91D Safir as the standard Finnish Air Force primary trainer and the first new military aircraft of Finnish design to fly since the Tuuli III primary trainer prototype of 1957, the Leko-70 is also envisaged as a touring aircraft with provision for a third seat at the rear of the cabin which may be removed to provide space for additional baggage. As a two-seater, the Leko-70 is fully aerobatic. Designed by the aeronautical research and development group at the Tampere works of the state-owned Valmet Oy, the Leko-70 was ordered as a prototype by the Finnish Air Force on March 23, 1973, and the data quoted above are based on design estimates and had still to be confirmed by the flight test programme at the time of closing for press.

VALMET LEKO-70

Dimensions: Span, 30 ft 6¼ in (9,30 m); length, 23 ft 11½ in (7,30 m); wing area, 150·69 sq ft (14,00 m²).

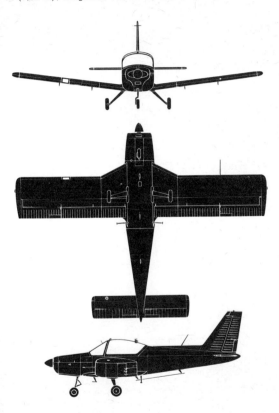

VFW-FOKKER VFW 614

Country of Origin: Federal Germany.
Type: Short-haul commercial transport.
Power Plant: Two 7,280 lb (3302 kg) Rolls-Royce/ SNECMA M45H Mk. 501 turbofans.
Performance: Max. speed, 457 mph (735 km/h) at 21,000 ft (6400 m); max. cruise, 449 mph (722 km/h) at 25,000 ft (7620 m); long-range cruise, 367 mph (591 km/h) at 25,000 ft (7620 m); max. fuel range (with reserves), 1,249 mls (2010 km); range (40 passengers and reserves), 748 mls (1205 km); max. climb, 3,100 ft/min (15,75 m/sec); service ceiling, 25,000 ft (7620 m).
Weights: Operational empty, 26,850 lb (12180 kg); max. take-off, 44,000 lb (19950 kg).
Accommodation: Basic flight crew of two and standard lay-out for 40 passengers in rows of four. Alternative arrangement for 44 passengers.
Status: First of three flying prototypes commenced test programme on July 14, 1971, with first production aircraft flying on April 28, 1975. This was delivered to Cimber Air in August 1975. Production of 30 authorised with orders and options for 10 (two for Cimber Air and eight on option for Touraine Air Transport) recorded by beginning of 1976.
Notes: Negotiations with the Romanian Government were proceeding late 1975 with a view to establishing an assembly line for the VFW 614 in Romania to supply East European customers. VFW 614 is a collaborative production programme under the leadership of VFW-Fokker, participants including the Dutch Fokker-VFW and Belgian SABCA and Fairey concerns.

VFW-FOKKER VFW 614

Dimensions: Span, 70 ft 6½ in (21,50 m); length, 67 ft 7 in (20,60 m); height, 25 ft 8 in (7,84 m); wing area, 688·89 sq ft (64,00 m²).

WSK-MIELEC M-15

Country of Origin: Poland.
Type: Three-seat agricultural biplane.
Power Plant: One 3,307 lb (1 500 kg) Ivchenko AI-25 turbofan.
Performance: Max. cruise, 124 mph (200 km/h); normal operating speed, 92–99 mph (145–160 km/h); max. range, 372 mls (600 km) at 9,850 ft (3 000 m); initial climb, 880 ft/min (4,48 m/sec).
Weights: Empty equipped, 6,393 lb (2 900 kg); max. take-off, 12,456 lb (5 650 kg).
Status: Aerodynamic prototype (LLP-M15) flown May 20, 1973, followed by first representative prototype on January 9, 1974. First batch of five of initial pre-production batch of 20 aircraft delivered to USSR for trials on April 26, 1975. Soviet Government reportedly has a requirement for up to 3,000 aircraft in this category.
Notes: The world's first turbine-powered biplane, the M-15 has been evolved by a joint Polish–Soviet team. The twin chemical containers between the wings have a combined capacity of 638 Imp gal (2 900 l) of liquid or 4,850 lb (2 200 kg) of dry chemicals. The M-15 is intended to supplant the Antonov An-2 biplane in the agricultural role.

WSK-MIELEC M-15

Dimensions: Span, 72 ft 0½ in (21,96 m); length, 41 ft 8¾ in (12,72 m); height, 17 ft 6½ in (5,34 m); wing area, 723·33 sq ft (67,20 m²).

YAKOVLEV YAK-40 (CODLING)

Country of Origin: USSR.

Type: Short-range commercial feederliner.

Power Plant: Three 3,307 lb (1 500 kg) Ivchenko AI-25 turbofans.

Performance: Max. speed, 373 mph (600 km/h) at sea level, 466 mph (750 km/h) at 17,000 ft (5 180 m); max. cruise, 342 mph (550 km/h) at 19,685 ft (6 000 m); econ. cruise, 310 mph (500 km/h) at 32,810 ft (10 000 m); range with 5,070-lb (2 300-kg) payload at econ. cruise, 620 mls (1 000 km), with 3,140-lb (1 425-kg) payload and max. fuel, 920 mls (1 480 km); initial climb, 2,000 ft/min (10,16 m/sec); service ceiling at max. loaded weight, 38,715 ft (11 800 m).

Weights: Empty equipped, 19,865–21,715 lb (9 010– 9 850 kg); normal take-off, 27,250–34,170 lb (12 360– 15 500 kg); max. take-off, 36,375 lb (16 500 kg).

Accommodation: Flight crew of two, and alternative arrangements for 27 or 34 passengers in three-abreast rows. High-density arrangement for 40 passengers in four-abreast rows, and executive configuration for 8–10 passengers.

Status: First of five prototypes flown October 21, 1966, and first production deliveries (to Aeroflot) mid-1968, the 500th example being completed on February 15, 1974.

Notes: A thrust reverser introduced as standard on centre engine during 1971 when more powerful version with three 3,858 lb (1 750 kg) AI-25T turbofans and increased fuel capacity was announced for 1974 delivery as the Yak-40V. This version has apparently been discontinued, but the uprated power plant is installed in Yak-40s serving in the liaison role with the Soviet Air Forces.

YAKOVLEV YAK-40 (CODLING)

Dimensions: Span, 82 ft 0¼ in (25,00 m); length, 66 ft 9½ in (20,36 m); height, 21 ft 4 in (6,50 m); wing area, 753·473 sq ft (70 m²).

YAKOVLEV YAK-42

Country of Origin: USSR.

Type: Short- to medium-haul commercial transport.

Power Plant: Three 14,200 lb (6 440 kg) Lotarev D-36 turbofans.

Performance: Max. cruise, 528 mph (850 km/h) at 32,810 ft (10 000 m); econ. cruise, 503 mph (810 km/h) at 26,250 ft (8 000 m); range with max. payload (30,850 lb/14 000 kg), 1,118 mls (1 800 km), with max. fuel, 1,740 mls (2,800 km); time to cruise altitude (26,250 ft/8 000 m), 11 min.

Weights: Max. take-off, 110,230 lb (50 000 kg).

Accommodation: Flight crew of two and standard single-class six-abreast seating for 102 passengers. Alternative arrangement for 120 passengers.

Status: First of three prototypes flown on March 7, 1975. Manufacturer's flight trials completed in September 1975, with initial services scheduled to be flown by Aeroflot during 1977.

Notes: Intended for operation over stages ranging from 248 mls (400 km) to 1,678 mls (2 700 km) and utilising restricted airfields with poor surfaces and limited facilities in the remoter areas of the Soviet Union in temperatures ranging from −50°C to +50°C, the Yak-42 is independent of airport ground equipment and a heavy-duty undercarriage caters for relatively rough strips. Retaining a close family resemblance to the earlier and smaller Yak-40, the Yak-42 can take-off from airfields no larger than those required for the previously-mentioned aircraft. Aeroflot reportedly possesses a requirement for up to 2,000 aircraft in the Yak-42 category in the 1980–90 timescale.

YAKOVLEV YAK-42

Dimensions: Span, 114 ft 10 in (35,00 m); length, 114 ft 10 in (35,00 m).

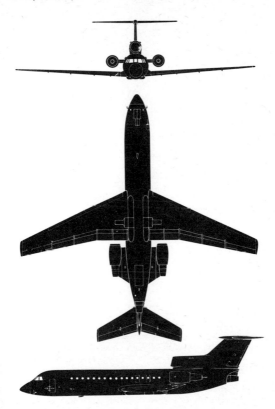

AÉROSPATIALE SA 315B LAMA

Country of Origin: France.
Type: Five-seat light utility helicopter.
Power Plant: One 870 shp (derated to 550 shp) Turboméca Artouste IIIB turboshaft.
Performance: Max. speed, 130 mph (210 km/h) at sea level; max. cruise, 119 mph (192 km/h), with slung load, 75 mph (120 km/h); max. inclined climb rate, 1,319 ft/min (6,7 m/sec); hovering ceiling (in ground effect), 8,530 ft (2 600 m), (out of ground effect), 1,312 ft (400 m); range (at 3,858 lb/1 750 kg), 317 mls (510 km) at sea level, 373 mls (600 km) at 9,840 ft (3 000 m).
Weights: Empty, 2,193 lb (995 kg); max. take-off, 4,850 lb (2 200 kg).
Dimensions: Rotor diam, 36 ft 1¾ in (11,02 m); fuselage length, 33 ft 8 in (10,26 m).
Notes: Flown for the first time on March 17, 1969, the Lama combines features of the SA 318C Alouette II (see 1973 edition) and the SA 319A Alouette III (see 1974 edition), having the airframe of the former (with some reinforcement) and the dynamic components of the latter. Developed primarily to meet the requirements of the Indian armed forces, the Lama is manufactured under licence by Hindustan Aeronautics as the Cheetah (illustrated above). The Lama can transport an external load of 2,204 lb (1 000 kg) at an altitude of more than 8,200 ft (2 500 m).

AÉROSPATIALE SA 330 PUMA

Country of Origin: France.
Type: Medium transport helicopter.
Power Plant: Two 1,320 shp Turboméca Turmo III C4 turbo-shafts.
Performance: Max. Speed, 174 mph (280 km/h) at sea level; max. cruise, 165 mph (265 km/h); max. inclined climb, 1,400 ft/min (7,1 m/sec); hovering ceiling (in ground effect), 9,186 ft (2 800 m), (out of ground effect), 6,233 ft (1 900 m); max. range, 390 mls (630 km).
Weights: Empty, 7,561 lb (3 430 kg); max. take-off, 14,110 (6 400 kg).
Dimensions: Rotor diam, 49 ft 2½ on (15,00 m), fuselage length, 46 ft 1½ in (14,06 m).
Notes: The Puma is being built under a joint production agreement between Aérospatiale and Westland, the first to be assembled by the latter concern flying on November 25, 1970. The Puma can accommodate 16–20 troops or up to 5,511 lb (2 500 kg) of cargo, and 40 have been delivered to the RAF for the assault role, 130 having been ordered by French Army Aviation. The Puma has been supplied to the Portuguese, South African, Zaïre Rep., Abu Dhabian, Algerian, and Ivory Coast air arms, and a commercial version, the SA 330F (illustrated above) with 1,385 shp Turmo IVA turbo-shafts, obtained FAA Type Approval in 1971, this carrying 15–17 passengers over 217 mls (350 km).

AÉROSPATIALE SA 341 GAZELLE

Country of Origin: France.
Type: Five-seat light utility helicopter.
Power Plant: One 592 shp Turboméca Astazou IIIA turboshaft.
Performance: Max. speed, 165 mph (265 km/h) at sea level; max. cruise, 149 mph (240 km/h); max. inclined climb rate, 1,214 ft/min (6,16 m/sec); hovering ceiling (in ground effect), 10,170 ft (3 100 m), (out of ground effect), 8,530 ft (2 600 m); max. range, 403 mls (650 km).
Weights: Empty, 1,873 lb (850 kg); max. take-off, 3,747 lb (1 700 kg).
Dimensions: Rotor diam, 34 ft $5\frac{1}{2}$ in (10,50 m); fuselage length, 31 ft $2\frac{3}{4}$ in (9,52 m).
Notes: Intended as a successor to the Alouette II, the Gazelle is being built under a joint production agreement between Aérospatiale and Westland. Two prototypes and four pre-production Gazelles were flown, and the first production example flew on August 6, 1971. The Gazelle is operated in the LOH (Light Observation Helicopter) role by both the French (SA 341F) and British armed forces (SA 341B for the Army, SA 341C for the Navy and SA 341D for the RAF), and it is anticipated that these will respectively purchase some 170 and 250 Gazelles. Licence production is being undertaken in Yugoslavia and deliveries commenced late 1973.

AÉROSPATIALE SA 350

Country of Origin: France.

Type: Experimental light utility helicopter.

Power Plant: One 600 shp Avco Lycoming LTS 101-650C turboshaft.

Performance: Max. cruise, 143 mph (230 km/h); max. range (with five passengers), 480 mls (775 km).

Weights: Max. take-off, 4,190 lb (1 900 kg).

Dimensions: No details available for publication.

Notes: Flown as a prototype for the first time on June 27, 1974, the five-to-six seat SA 350 is a beneficiary of research and development funding provided in the 1975—76 French civil aviation budget. Few details of the SA 350 have yet been revealed, but it has been reported that Aérospatiale is proposing the extensive use of plastics in the construction of derivatives of the basic design, and is considering a number of alternative engines, including Wankel-type rotating piston engines. Envisaged as a potential successor to the Alouette II Astazou and Lama light general-purpose helicopters, the SA 350 is being developed for both civil and military roles, and reference has been made to a single-engined SA 370 and a twin-engined SA 375 as possible production versions of the basic design. However, although the SA 350 prototype had been under test for some 18 months by the beginning of 1976, production is unlikely before the late 'seventies.

AÉROSPATIALE SA 360 DAUPHIN

Country of Origin: France.

Type: Multi-purpose and transport helicopter.

Power Plant: One 1,025 shp (derated to 878 shp) Turbo-méca Astazou XVIIIA turboshaft.

Performance: Max. cruise, 171 mph (275 km/h); econ. cruise, 143 mph (230 km/h); inclined climb rate (at 5,500 lb/2 500 kg), 1,476 ft/min (7,5 m/sec); hovering ceiling (in ground effect), 15,584 ft (4 750 m), (out of ground effect), 14,107 ft (4 300 m); range (with 2,204-lb/1 000-kg payload), 62 mls (100 km), (with 1,323-lb/600-kg payload), 466 mls (750 km).

Weights: Empty equipped, 2,976 lb (1 350 kg); max. take-off, 5,952 lb (2 700 kg).

Dimensions: Rotor diam, 37 ft 8¾ in (11,50 m); fuselage length, 36 ft 4 in (11,08 m).

Notes: Intended as a successor to the Alouette III, the SA 360 utilises a semi-rigid four-blade rotor and a ducted 11-blade tail rotor. The two prototypes made their initial flights on June 2, 1972, and January 29, 1973, respectively, and the first production example was flown in April 1975, and it was anticipated that initial customer deliveries would be made in the spring of 1976. The SA 360 version of the Dauphin provides accommodation for a flight crew of two and eight passengers, an ambulance version carrying four casualty stretchers and a medical attendant.

226

AÉROSPATIALE SA 365 DAUPHIN

Country of Origin: France.
Type: Multi-purpose and transport helicopter.
Power Plant: Two 650 shp Turboméca Arriel turboshafts.
Performance: (At 5,510 lb/2 500 kg) Max. cruise, 162 mph (260 km/h); econ. cruise, 146 mph (235 km/h); max. inclined climb, 1,810 ft/min (9,19 m/sec); hovering ceiling (in ground effect), 15,000 ft (4 575 m), (out of ground effect), 15,000 ft (4 575 m); max. range at econ. cruise, 376 mls (605 km).
Weights: Max. take-off, 7,055 lb (3 200 kg).
Dimensions: Main rotor diam, 37 ft 8¾ in (11,50 m); fuselage length, 36 ft 3⅜ in (11,07 m).
Notes: The SA 365 is a development of the basic Dauphin (see opposite page) with twin engines, the prototype having flown on January 24, 1975, and a variant, the SA 366 with twin Avco Lycoming LTS 101 turboshafts, flew a few days later, on January 28. Aérospatiale has no plans to develop the SA 366 further, but production deliveries of the SA 365 are scheduled to commence during the second half of 1977, the first announced sale being to Air Taxi of Anchorage, Alaska. Like the SA 360, the SA 365 normally accommodates a flight crew of either one or two and eight to nine passengers. Executive versions are available with VIP interiors for four or five passengers, and the SA 365 is being offered for military roles and may be fitted with Minitat gun turret and HOT missiles for the gunship task.

227

AGUSTA A 109C HIRUNDO

Country of Origin: Italy.

Type: Eight-seat utility helicopter.

Power Plant: Two 400 shp Allison 250-C20 turboshafts.

Performance: (At 4,850 lb/2 200 kg) Max. speed, 169 mph (272 km/h) at sea level; econ. cruise, 139 mph (223 km/h) at sea level; max. inclined climb, 2,067 ft/min (10,5 m/sec); hovering ceiling (in ground effect), 11,810 ft (3 600 m), (out of ground effect), 9,190 ft (2 800 m); max. range, 457 mls (735 km) at 6,560 ft (2 000 m).

Weights: Empty, 2,645 lb (1 200 kg); max. take-off, 5,291 lb (2 400 kg).

Dimensions: Rotor diam, 36 ft 1 in (11,00 m); fuselage length, 36 ft 7 in (11,14 m).

Notes: The first of four Hirundo (Swallow) prototypes flew on August 4, 1971. This was lost as a result of resonance problems, flight trials being resumed with the second and third prototypes early 1973. The first production examples were delivered late in 1975, at which time an initial batch of 10 was being built. The Hirundo is intended to fit between the licence-built Bell 206 JetRanger and Bell 212 in the Agusta helicopter range, and carries a pilot and seven passengers in its basic form. It is also suitable for the ambulance role, accommodating two casualty stretchers and two medical attendants when the forward cabin bulkhead is removed, and for freight carrying the forward row of passenger seats may be removed.

BELL MODEL 205A-1 (IROQUOIS)

Country of Origin: USA.

Type: Fifteen-seat utility helicopter.

Power Plant: One 1,400 shp Lycoming T5313A turboshaft.

Performance: (At 9,500 lb/4 309 kg) Max. speed, 127 mph (204 km/h) at sea level; max. cruise, 111 mph (179 km/h) at 8,000 ft (2 440 m); max. inclined climb, 1,680 ft/min (8,53 m/sec); hovering ceiling (in ground effect), 10,400 ft (3 170 m), (out of ground effect), 6,000 ft (1 830 m); range, 344 mls (553 km) at 8,000 ft (2 440 m).

Weights: Empty equipped, 5,082 lb (2 305 kg); normal take-off, 9,500 lb (4 309 kg).

Dimensions: Rotor diam, 48 ft 0 in (14,63 m); fuselage length, 41 ft 6 in (12,65 m).

Notes: The Model 205A is basically similar to the Model 204B (see 1973 edition) but introduces a longer fuselage with increased cabin space. It is produced under licence in Italy by Agusta as the AB 205, and is assembled under licence in Formosa (Taiwan). The initial version for the US Army, the UH-1D, had a 1,100 shp T53-L-11 turboshaft. This model was manufactured under licence in Federal Germany. The UH-1D has been succeeded in production for the US Army by the UH-1H with a 1,400 shp T53-L-13 turboshaft, and a similar helicopter for the Mobile Command of the Canadian Armed Forces is designated CUH-1H. A progressive development is the Model 214 (see page 234).

BELL MODEL 206B JETRANGER II

Country of Origin: USA.
Type: Five-seat light utility helicopter.
Power Plant: One 400 shp Allison 250-C20 turboshaft.
Performance: (At 3,000 lb/1 361 kg) Max. cruise, 136 mph (219 km/h) at sea level, 142 mph (228 km/h) at 5,000 ft (1 524 m); hovering ceiling (in ground effect), 13,200 ft (4 023 m), (out of ground effect), 8,700 ft (2 652 m); max. inclined climb, 1,540 ft/min (7,82 m/sec); max. range, 436 mls (702 km) at 10,000 ft (3 048 m).
Weights: Empty, 1,455 lb (660 kg); max. take-off, 3,000 lb (1 360 kg).
Dimensions: Rotor diam, 33 ft 4 in (10,16 m); fuselage length, 31 ft 2 in (9,50 m).
Notes: The JetRanger is manufactured in both commercial and military versions, and the current production variant, the Model 206B JetRanger II, differs from the Model 206A Jet-Ranger in having an uprated turboshaft. A light observation version for the US Army is known as the OH-58A Kiowa, and a training version for the US Navy is known as the TH-57A SeaRanger. An Australian-built version of the Model 206B is being delivered to the Australian Army, and this helicopter is also built in Italy by Agusta as the AB 206B-1. The OH-58A Kiowa has a larger main rotor of 35 ft 4 in (10,77 m) diameter and a fuselage of 32 ft 3½ in (9,84 m) length.

BELL MODEL 206L LONG RANGER

Country of Origin: USA.
Type: Seven-seat light utility helicopter.
Power Plant: One 420 shp Allison 250-C20B turboshaft.
Performance: (At 3,900 lb/1 769 kg) Max. speed, 144 mph (232 km/h); cruise, 136 mph (229 km/h) at sea level; hovering ceiling (in ground effect), 8,200 ft (2 499 m), (out of ground effect), 2,000 ft (610 m); range, 390 mls (628 km) at sea level, 430 mls (692 km) at 5,000 ft (1 524 m).
Weights: Empty, 1,861 lb (844 kg); max. take-off, 3,900 lb (1 769 kg).
Dimensions: Rotor diam. 37 ft 0 in (11,28 m); fuselage length, 33 ft 3 in (10,13 m).
Notes: The Model 206L Long Ranger is a stretched and more powerful version of the Model 206B JetRanger II, with a longer fuselage, increased fuel capacity, an uprated engine and a larger rotor. The Long Ranger is being manufactured in parallel with the JetRanger II and initial customer deliveries commenced late in 1975, prototype testing having been initiated during the course of 1973. The Long Ranger is available with emergency flotation gear and with a 2,000-lb (907-kg) capacity cargo hook. Cabin volume is 83 cu ft (2,35 m³) as compared with the 49 cu ft (1,39 m³) of the JetRanger II (see page 230). By 1976, some 4,500 commercial and military examples of the basic JetRanger series had been delivered. Licence manufacture is undertaken in Italy by Agusta.

BELL MODEL 209 HUEYCOBRA

Country of Origin: USA.

Type: Two-seat attack helicopter.

Power Plant: One 1,800 shp Pratt & Whitney (Canada) T400-CP-400 coupled turboshaft.

Performance: Max. speed, 207 mph (333 km/h) at sea level; max. range (without reserves, 359 mls (577 km); max. inclined climb, 1,090 ft/min (5,54 m/sec); hovering ceiling (in ground effect), 12,450 ft (3 794 m).

Weights: Operational (including crew), 6,816 lb (3 091 kg); max. take-off, 10,000 lb (4 535 kg).

Dimensions: Rotor diam, 44 ft 0 in (13,41 m); fuselage length, 44 ft 7 in (13,59 m).

Notes: The version of the Model 209 HueyCobra described above is employed by the US Marine Corps as the AH-1J SeaCobra, differing from the US Army's AH-1G primarily in having a "Twin Pac" power plant. One hundred and twenty-four AH-1Js are being procured by the USMC, of which 55 are to be of an improved version with a 1,970 shp T400-WV-402, and 202 examples are being supplied to Iran. By comparison with the AH-1G, the AH-1J has an improved armament system embodying a three-barrelled 20-mm XM-197 cannon in a chin turret. Four external stores attachment points under the stub-wings can carry a variety of ordnance loads, including Minigun pods and rocket packs. An Iranian example of the HueyCobra is illustrated above.

BELL MODEL 212 TWIN TWO-TWELVE

Country of Origin: USA.

Type: Fifteen-seat utility helicopter.

Power Plant: One 1,800 shp Pratt & Whitney PT6T-3 coupled turboshaft.

Performance: Max. speed, 121 mph (194 km/h) at sea level; max. inclined climb at 10,000 lb (4 535 kg), 1,460 ft/min (7,4 m/sec); hovering ceiling (in ground effect), 17,100 ft (5 212 m), (out of ground effect), 9,900 ft (3 020 m); max. range, 296 mls (476 km) at sea level.

Weights: Empty, 5,500 lb (2 495 kg); max. take-off, 10,000 lb (4 535 kg).

Dimensions: Rotor diam, 48 ft 2½ in (14,69 m); fuselage length, 42 ft 10¾ in (13,07 m).

Notes: The Model 212 is based on the Model 205 (see page 229) from which it differs primarily in having a twin-engined power plant (two turboshaft engines coupled to a combining gearbox with a single output shaft), and both commercial and military versions are being produced. A model for the Canadian Armed Forces is designated CUH-1N, and an essentially similar variant of the Model 212, the UH-1N, is being supplied to the USAF, the USN, and the USMC. All versions of the Model 212 can carry an external load of 4,400 lb (1 814 kg), and can maintain cruise performance on one engine component at maximum gross weight.

BELL MODEL 214

Country of Origin: USA.

Type: Sixteen-seat utility helicopter.

Power Plant: One 2,930 shp Avco Lycoming T55-L-7C turboshaft.

Performance: Max. speed, 190 mph (305 km/h) at sea level; max. cruise (at gross weight of 13,000 lb/5 897 kg), 150 mph (241 km/h); range, 300 mls (483 km).

Weights: Normal max. take-off, 13,000 lb (5 897 kg), (with slung load), 15,000 lb (6 804 kg).

Dimensions: Rotor diam, 50 ft 0 in (15,20 m).

Notes: Development of the Model 214, originally known as the HueyPlus, was initiated in 1970 as a progressive development of the Model 205 (UH-1H). Utilising an essentially similar airframe with strengthened main beams, pylon structure and aft fuselage, and the main rotor and tail rotor drive systems of the Model 309 KingCobra (see 1973 edition) coupled with the Lycoming T55-L-7C turboshaft installed in the second KingCobra, this utility helicopter is being developed for military use as the Model 214A and was certificated in 1975 for commercial use as the Model 214B (Avco Lycoming LTC4B-8D). First flight of the Model 214A took place on March 13, 1974, and first deliveries against orders from the Iranian Government for 287 helicopters of this type began in April 1975, and was building up to 10 per month at the beginning of 1976.

BELL MODEL 222

Country of Origin: USA.
Type: Light utility and transport helicopter.
Power Plant: Two 600 shp Avco Lycoming LTS 101-650C turboshafts.
Performance: (Estimated) Max. speed, 180 mph (290 km/h); long-range cruise, 150+ mph (240+ km/h); range (with 20 min reserves), 425 mls (684 km).
Weights: Empty, 3,930 lb (1 784 kg); max. take-off, 6,700 lb (3 042 kg).
Dimensions: Rotor diam, 39 ft 0 in (11,89 m); fuselage length, 39 ft 9 in (12,12 m).
Notes: Committed to full-scale development in March 1974 as "the first US-manufactured light twin-turbine helicopter", the Model 222 was expected to commence its flight test programme early in 1976, and current schedules call for the delivery of production models to commence in 1978. The Model 222 is designed to accommodate up to 10 (including pilot) in a high-density arrangement, the standard interior providing eight seats with an executive version accommodating pilot and five passengers. In the aeromedical role, two stretchers and two attendants will be accommodated in the cabin. A wide-chord, two-bladed rotor has been adopted, with swept tips, for low noise levels, and Bell's Nodamatic suspension system is used to reduce vibration. The undercarriage is fully retractable.

235

BELL MODEL 409 (YAH-63)

Country of Origin: USA.

Type: Tandem two-seat attack helicopter.

Power Plant: Two 1,536 shp General Electric T700-GE-700 turboshafts.

Performance: (Estimated) Max. speed, 200 mph (322 km/h) at 4,000 ft (1 220 m); max. cruise, 178 mph (286 km/h); max range (internal fuel), 300 mls (483 km).

Weights: Normal mission gross, 13,500 lb (6 124 kg).

Dimensions: No details available for publication.

Notes: The Model 409 is one of two designs selected by the US Army for competitive evaluation for selection as the service's AAH (Advanced Attack Helicopter), a contract for two flying prototypes and a ground test specimen having been placed on June 22, 1973, under the designation YAH-63, the competitor being the Hughes YAH-64 (see page 239). The first prototype YAH-63 commenced its flight test programme on October 1, 1975, and both prototypes are scheduled to be delivered to the US Army by May 31, 1976, for the competitive fly-off, the winner of which is to be announced by the end of 1976. The US Army has outline plans for the acquisition of 472 AAHs. The YAH-63 embodies extensive armour, blast-proof glass shields separating the cockpits and a turret-mounted triple-barrel 30-mm XM-188 rotary cannon, the gunner being housed in the aft cockpit. Up to eight TOW missiles may be carried.

BOEING VERTOL MODEL 114

Country of Origin: USA.
Type: Medium transport helicopter.
Power Plant: (CH-47C) Two 3,750 shp Lycoming T55-L-11 turboshafts.
Performance: (CH-47C at 33,000 lb/14 969 kg) Max. speed, 190 mph (306 km/h) at sea level; average cruise, 158 mph (254 km/h); max. inclined climb, 2,880 ft/min (14,63 m/sec); hovering ceiling (out of ground effect), 14,750 ft (4 495 m); mission radius, 115 mls (185 km).
Weights: Empty, 20,378 lb (9 243); max. take-off, 46,000 lb (20 865 kg).
Dimensions: Rotor diam (each), 60 ft 0 in (18,29 m); fuselage length, 51 ft 0 in (15,54 m).
Notes: The Model 114 is the standard medium transport helicopter of the US Army, and is operated by that service under the designation CH-47 Chinook. The initial production model, the CH-47A, was powered by 2,200 shp T55-L-5 or 2,650 shp T55-L-7 turboshafts. This was succeeded by the CH-47B with 2,850 shp T55-L-7C engines, redesigned rotor blades and other modifications, and this, in turn, gave place to the current CH-47C with more powerful engines, strengthened transmissions, and increased fuel capacity. This model is manufactured in Italy by Elicotteri Meriodionali, orders calling for 24 (of 26) for the Italian Army and 18 (of 42) for the Iranian Army.

BOEING VERTOL MODEL 179 (YUH-61A)

Country of Origin: USA.
Type: Tactical transport helicopter.
Power Plant: Two 1,536 shp General Electric YT700-GE-700 turboshafts.
Performance: Max. cruise, 180 mph (290 km/h); econ. cruise, 154 mph (216 km/h); range (no reserves), 598 mls (964 km) at 5,000 ft (1 525 m).
Weights: Max. take-off, 18,700 lb (8 482 kg).
Dimensions: Rotor diam., 49 ft 0 in (14,93 m); fuselage length, 51 ft 8¾ in (15,77 m).
Notes: The YUH-61A is one of two finalists in the US Army's UTTAS (Utility Tactical Transport Aircraft System) contest, one static test example and three flying prototypes having been ordered, the first of the latter having flown on November 29, 1974. A fourth flying prototype has been built as a company-owned demonstrator, the Boeing Vertol Company planning to market a commercial 14–25 passenger version. The YUH-61A is competing with the Sikorsky YUH-60A (see page 247) as a successor to the Bell UH-1H Iroquois in the troop transportation, casevac and logistics support roles, and a competitive evaluation of the two helicopter types was being conducted by the US Army from late 1975 with the aim of selecting one for production from March 1977. The YUH-61A can carry a 10,000-lb (4 536 kg) slung load and is transportable by C-130 Hercules.

238

HUGHES YAH-64

Country of Origin: USA.

Type: Tandem two-seat attack helicopter.

Power Plant: Two 1,536 shp General Electric T700-GE-700 turboshafts.

Performance: (Estimated) Max. speed, 191 mph (307 km/h) at sea level; max. cruise, 180 mph (290 km/h); hovering ceiling (in ground effect), 14,600 ft (4 450 m), (out of ground effect), 11,800 ft (3 597 m); max. range, 359 mls (578 km).

Weights: (Estimated) Primary mission, 13,200 lb (5 987 kg); max. take-off, 17,400 lb (7 892 kg).

Dimensions: Rotor diam, 48 ft 0 in (14,63 m).

Notes: Competing with the Bell YAH-63 (see page 236) for selection as the US Army's AAH (Advanced Attack Helicopter), the YAH-64 was flown for the first time on September 30, 1975, and will participate in a side by side fly off with the Bell contender from May 1976. Three additional prototypes of the successful AAH will be ordered for avionics and weapons fire control system development. Smaller and lighter than the YAH-63, the YAH-64 has a single-barrel 30-mm gun, which, based on the chain-driven bolt system, is suspended beneath the forward fuselage, the gunner occupying the forward cockpit. For the primary mission, the YAH-64 will carry eight BGM-71A TOW (Tube-launched Optically-tracked Wire-guided) anti-armour missiles. The second prototype of the Hughes AAH was flown on November 22, 1975.

KAMOV KA-25 (HORMONE A)

Country of Origin: USSR.
Type: Shipboard anti-submarine warfare helicopter.
Power Plant: Two 900 shp Glushenkov GTD-3 turboshafts.
Performance: (Estimated) Max. speed, 130 mph (209 km/h); normal cruise, 120 mph (193 km/h); max. range, 400 mls (644 km); service ceiling, 11,000 ft (3 353 m).
Weights: (Estimated) Empty, 10,500 lb (4 765 kg); max. take-off, 16,500 lb (7 484 kg).
Dimensions: Rotor diam (each), 51 ft 7$\frac{1}{2}$ in (15,74 m); approx. fuselage length, 35 ft 6 in (10,82 m).
Notes: Possessing a basically similar airframe to that of the Ka-25K (see 1973 edition) and employing a similar self-contained assembly comprising rotors, transmission, engines and auxiliaries, the Ka-25 serves with the Soviet Navy primarily in the ASW role but is also employed in the utility and transport roles. The ASW Ka-25 serves aboard the helicopter cruisers *Moskva* and *Leningrad* as well as with shore-based units. A search radar installation is mounted in a nose radome, but other sensor housings and antennae differ widely from helicopter to helicopter. There is no evidence that externally-mounted weapons may be carried. Each landing wheel is surrounded by an inflatable pontoon surmounted by inflation bottles. Sufficient capacity is available to accommodate up to a dozen personnel. The commercial Ka-25K can be employed in the flying crane role.

MBB BO 105

Country of Origin: Federal Germany.
Type: Five/six-seat light utility helicopter.
Power Plant: Two 400 shp Allison 250-C20 turboshafts.
Performance: Max. speed, 155 mph (250 km/h) at sea level; max. cruise, 138 mph (222 km/h); max. inclined climb, 1,870 ft/min (9,5 m/sec); hovering ceiling (in ground effect), 7,610 ft (2 320 m), (out of ground effect), 5,085 ft (1 550 m); normal range, 388 mls (625 km) at 5,000 ft (1 525 m).
Weights: Empty, 2,360 lb (1 070 kg); normal take-off, 4,630 lb (2 100 kg); max. take-off, 5,070 lb (2 300 kg).
Dimensions: Rotor diam, 32 ft 1¾ in (9,80 m); fuselage length, 28 ft 0½ in (8,55 m).
Notes: The BO 105 features a rigid unarticulated main rotor with folding glass-fibre reinforced plastic blades, and the first prototype (with a conventional rotor) was tested in 1966, three prototypes being followed by four pre-production examples, and production deliveries commencing during 1971. The German armed forces have acquired examples for evaluation. The third prototype was powered by 375 shp MTU 6022 turboshafts, but the production model has standardised on the Allison 250. Production is undertaken by the Siebelwerke-ATG subsidiary of MBB and some 240 BO 105s had been flown by the beginning of 1976. A seven-seat derivative, the BO 106, was flown on September 25, 1973.

MIL MI-8 (HIP)

Country of Origin: USSR.
Type: General-purpose transport helicopter.
Power Plant: Two 1,500 shp Isotov TV-2-117A turboshafts.
Performance: (At 24,470 lb/11 100 kg) Max. speed, 155 mph (250 km/h); max. cruise, 140 mph (225 km/h); hovering ceiling (in ground effect), 5,900 ft (1 800 m), (out of ground effect), 2,625 ft (800 m); service ceiling, 14,760 ft (4 500 m); range with 6,615 lb (3 000 kg) of freight, 264 mls (425 km).
Weights: Empty (cargo), 15,787 lb (7 171 kg), (passenger), 16,352 lb (7 417 kg); normal take-off, 24,470 lb (11 100 kg); max. take-off (for VTO), 26,455 lb (12 000 kg).
Dimensions: Rotor diam, 69 ft 10$\frac{1}{4}$ in (21,29 m); fuselage length, 59 ft 7$\frac{1}{2}$ in (18,17 m).
Notes: The Mi-8 has been in continuous production since 1964 for both civil and military tasks. The standard commercial passenger version has a basic flight crew of two or three and 28 four-abreast seats, and the aeromedical version accommodates 12 casualty stretchers and a medical attendant. As a freighter the Mi-8 will carry up to 8,818 lb (4 000 kg) of cargo, and military tasks include assault transport, search and rescue, and anti-submarine warfare. The Mi-8 is now operated by several Warsaw Pact air forces, serving primarily in the support transport role, and has been exported to numerous countries, including Finland, Pakistan and Egypt.

242

MIL MI-24 (HIND)

Country of Origin: USSR.
Type: Gunship and assault transport helicopter.
Power Plant: Two 1,500 shp Isotov TV-2-117A turboshafts.
Performance: (Estimated) Max. speed, 160 mph (257 km/h); max. cruise, 140 mph (225 km/h); hovering ceiling (in ground effect), 6,000 ft (1 830 m), (out of ground effect), 1,600 ft (790 m); normal range, 300 mls (480 km).
Weights: Normal loaded, 25,000 lb (11 340 kg).
Dimensions: Rotor diam., 55 ft 0 in (16,76 m); fuselage length, 55 ft 6 in (16,90 m).
Notes: Employed in considerable numbers by the Soviet forces, the Mi-24 is apparently serving in two versions. One version (*Hind-A*), illustrated above, has three weapons stations on each auxiliary wing, the two inboard stations carrying UV-32-57 rocket pods and the outboard station taking the form of a vertical extension of the wingtip with a double carrier for two AT-3 *Sagger* wire-guided anti-tank missiles. The other version (*Hind-B*) does not have the wingtip vertical extensions. Both versions have a 12,7-mm machine gun in the extreme fuselage nose, armour protection for the flight crew and accommodation for 8–12 assault troops with a large door aft of the flight deck on each side enabling them to exit rapidly. The Mi-24 may utilise some of the components of the Mi-8 (see opposite page) but appears to be somewhat smaller.

243

SIKORSKY S-61D (SEA KING)

Country of Origin: USA.

Type: Amphibious anti-submarine helicopter.

Power Plant: Two 1,500 shp General Electric T58-GE-10 turboshafts.

Performance: Max. speed, 172 mph (277 km/h) at sea level; inclined climb, 2,200 ft/min (11,2 m/sec); hovering ceiling (out of ground effect), 8,200 ft (2 500 m); range (with 10% reserves), 622 mls (1 000 km).

Weights: Empty equipped, 12,087 lb (5 481 kg); max. take-off, 20,500 lb (9 297 kg).

Dimensions: Rotor diam, 62 ft 0 in (18,90 m); fuselage length, 54 ft 9 in (16,69 m).

Notes: A more powerful derivative of the S-61B, the S-61D serves with the US Navy as the SH-3D, 74 helicopters of this type following on production of 255 SH-3As (S-61Bs) for the ASW role. Licence manufacture of the S-61D (with 1,500 shp Rolls-Royce Gnome turboshafts) is undertaken in the UK by Westland as the Sea King HAS Mk. 1, 56 being delivered to the Royal Navy. Deliveries of the improved Sea King Mk. 50 for the Royal Australian Navy began during the autumn of 1974, and production is being undertaken of a tactical transport version, the Commando (see page 249). Licence manufacture of the S-61D is also being undertaken in Italy by Agusta for the Italian and Iranian navies. The SH-3G and SH-3H are upgraded conversions of the SH-3A.

SIKORSKY S-61R

Country of Origin: USA.

Type: Amphibious transport and rescue helicopter.

Power Plant: (CH-3E) Two 1,500 shp General Electric T58-GE-5 turboshafts

Performance: (CH-3E at 21,247 lb/9 635 kg) Max. speed, 162 mph (261 km/h) at sea level; range cruise, 144 mph (232 km/h); max. inclined climb, 1,310 ft/min (6,6 m/sec); hovering ceiling (in ground effect), 4,100 ft (1 250 m); range with 10% reserves, 465 mls (748 km).

Weights: (CH-3E) Empty, 13,255 lb (6 010 kg); normal take-off, 21,247 lb (9 635 kg); max. take-off, 22,050 lb (10 000 kg).

Dimensions: Rotor diam, 62 ft 0 in (18,90 m); fuselage length, 57 ft 3 in (17,45 m).

Notes: Although based on the S-61A, the S-61R embodies numerous design changes, including a rear ramp and a tricycle-type undercarriage. Initial model for the USAF was the CH-3C with 1,300 shp T58-GE-1 turboshafts, but this was subsequently updated to CH-3E standards. The CH-3E can accommodate 25–30 troops or 5,000 lb (2 270 kg) of cargo, and may be fitted with a TAT-102 barbette on each sponson mounting a 7,62-mm Minigun. The HH-3E is a USAF rescue version with armour, self-sealing tanks, and refuelling probe, and the HH-3F Pelican (illustrated) is a US Coast Guard search and rescue model.

245

SIKORSKY S-65 (YCH-53E)

Country of Origin: USA.

Type: Amphibious assault transport helicopter.

Power Plant: Three 4,380 shp General Electric T64-GE-415 turboshafts.

Performance: Max. speed, 196 mph (315 km/h) at sea level; max. cruise, 173 mph (278 km/h).

Weights: Operational empty, 33,000 lb (14 968 kg); max. take-off, 69,750 lb (31 638 kg).

Dimensions: Rotor diam., 79 ft 0 in (24,08 m); fuselage length, 73 ft 5 in (22,38 m).

Notes: The YCH-53E is a growth version of the CH-53D Sea Stallion (see 1974 edition) embodying a third engine, an uprated transmission system, a seventh main rotor blade and increased rotor diameter. The first of two prototypes was flown on March 1, 1974, and the first of two pre-production prototypes flew on December 8, 1975, but a production decision was not anticipated prior to mid-1976. The YCH-53E can accommodate up to 56 troops in a high-density arrangement and can lift a 32,000-lb (14 515-kg) external load over a radius of 58 miles (93 km) at sea level in a 90 deg F temperature. The planned production programme envisages the acquisition of 70 helicopters of this type divided equally between the US Navy and US Marine Corps. The YCH-53E offers a major performance advance and can retrieve 93 per cent of USMC tactical aircraft without disassembly.

SIKORSKY S-70 (YUH-60A)

Country of Origin: USA.
Type: Tactical transport helicopter.
Power Plant: Two 1,536 shp General Electric YT700-GE-700 turboshafts.
Performance: (Estimated) Max. speed, 200 mph (322 km/h) at sea level; cruise, 184 mph (296 km/h); hovering ceiling (in ground effect), 10,000 ft (3 048 m), (out of ground effect), 6,800 ft (1 768 m); normal range, 400 mls (740 km).
Weights: Design gross, 16,500 lb (7 485 kg); max. take-off, 22,000 lb (9 979 kg).
Dimensions: Rotor diam, 53 ft 0 in (16,15 m); fuselage length, 50 ft 11½ in (15,53 m).
Notes: The YUH-64 was scheduled to participate in a fly-off with the competitive Boeing Vertol YUH-61A (see page 238) from early 1976, to enable the US Army to select a UTTAS (Utility Tactical Transport Aircraft System). The choice of a UTTAS is scheduled for November 1976, an initial contract for 15 examples of the winning helicopter being placed with deliveries commencing July 1978. The first of three YUH-60As was flown on October 17, 1974, and a company-funded fourth prototype flew on May 23, 1975, this being a demonstrator for the S-78-20, a commercial version of the YUH-60A with accommodation for 20 passengers, a projected developed version being the S-78-29.

SIKORSKY S-76

Country of Origin: USA.

Type: Fourteen-seat commercial transport helicopter.

Power Plant: Two 650 shp Allison 250-C30 turboshafts.

Performance: (Estimated at 8,400 lb/3 810 kg) Max. cruise, 178 mph (286 km/h); hovering ceiling (in ground effect), 9,000 ft (2 743 m); range (with 12 passengers and 30 min reserves), 461 mls (742 km); max. ferry range, 864 mls (1 390 km).

Weights: Empty equipped, 4,804 lb (2 179 kg); max. take-off, 9,700 lb (4 399 kg).

Dimensions: Rotor diam, 40 ft 0 in (12,19 m); fuselage length, 41 ft 10 in (12,75 m).

Notes: Scheduled to commence its flight test programme mid-1976, with quantity production planned to commence in 1978, the S-76 is unique among Sikorsky helicopters in that conceptually it owes nothing to an existing military model. Although aimed at the commercial market, the S-76 is being built to conform with appropriate military specifications so that it may be taken "off the shelf" to satisfy a military role without major modifications to airframe structure or dynamic system. To accommodate pilot, co-pilot and a maximum of 12 passengers, the S-76 is also to be offered with various executive layouts for four or six passengers. An optional external cargo hook will have a capacity of 5,000 lb (2 268 kg).

WESTLAND COMMANDO MK. 2

Country of Origin: United Kingdom (US licence).
Type: Tactical transport helicopter.
Power Plant: Two 1,590 shp Rolls-Royce Gnome 1400-1 turboshafts.
Performance: Max. speed (at 19,900 lb/9 046 kg), 138 mph (222 km/h); max. cruise, 127 mph (204 km/h); max. inclined climb, 1,930 ft/min (9,8 m/sec); range (with 30 troops), 161 mls (259 km); ferry range, 1,036 mls (1 668 km).
Weights: Empty equipped, 11,487–12,122 lb (5 221–5 510 kg); max. take-off, 20,000 lb (9 072 kg).
Dimensions: Rotor diam, 62 ft 0 in (18,89 m); fuselage length, 54 ft 9 in (16,69 m).
Notes: The Commando is a Westland-developed land-based army support helicopter derivative of the licence-built Sikorsky S-61D Sea King (see page 244), search radar and other specialised items being deleted together with the sponsons which endow the Sea King with amphibious capability. The first five examples completed as Commando Mk. 1s were minimum change conversions of Sea King airframes, the first of these flying on September 12, 1973, but subsequent Commandos are being built to Mk. 2 standards with the uprated Gnome turboshafts selected for the Sea King Mk. 50s ordered by Australia. The first production deliveries (to Egypt) commenced in 1975.

WESTLAND WG.13 LYNX

Country of Origin: United Kingdom.
Type: Multi-purpose and transport helicopter.
Power Plant: Two 900 shp Rolls-Royce BS.360-07-26 turboshafts.
Performance: (General-purpose version) Max. cruise, 170 mph (273 km/h); max. inclined climb, 2,198 ft/min (11,16 m/sec); hovering ceiling (out of ground effect), 12,000 ft (3 650 m); max. range, 420 mls (676 km).
Weights: Operational empty, 5,914–6,693 lb (2 682–3 036 kg); max. take-off, 9,500 lb (4 309 kg).
Dimensions: Rotor diam, 42 ft 0 in (12,80 m); fuselage length, 39 ft 6⅝ in (12,06 m).
Notes: The Lynx, the first of 13 development aircraft having flown on March 21, 1971, is scheduled to enter service with the British Army during the autumn of 1976 as the Lynx AH Mk. 1, deliveries commencing during the course of the year to the Royal Navy as the Lynx HAS Mk. 2. The latter is intended for shipborne anti-submarine duties and features Ferranti Seaspray search and tracking radar and provision for two Mk. 44 or Mk. 46 torpedoes, or two Mk. 11 depth charges. A version generally similar to the HAS Mk. 2 is to be supplied to the French Navy (which has a requirement for 80 examples), and a civil version of the Lynx, the Westland 606, is under development, this providing accommodation for a flight crew of two and 12–13 passengers.

ACKNOWLEDGEMENTS

The author wishes to record his thanks to the following sources of copyright photographs appearing in this volume: Aviation Photo News, page 218; M. Balous, page 242; Flug Revue, pages 160, 243; Howard Levy, pages 36, 82, 234; S. Peltz, pages 20, 92, 192; Tass, page 220. The three-view silhouettes published in this volume are copyright Pilot Press Limited and may not be reproduced without prior permission.

INDEX OF AIRCRAFT TYPES

Printed for the Publishers by
Butler & Tanner Ltd, Frome and London

0605.1175